To God Be The Glory

I0307908

To God Be The Glory

52 of the
Greatest Song Stories
Ever Told

Lindsay Terry

AMG
PUBLISHERS
ADVANCING THE MINISTRIES OF THE GOSPEL

To God Be the Glory:
52 of the Greatest Song Stories Ever Told

ISBN: 978-1-61715-486-7
First Printing, 2016

Cover Design, Book Design and Editing by AMG Publishers

Printed in the United States of America
22 21 20 19 18 17 16 –AZ– 7 6 5 4 3 2 1

Table of Contents

Preface

The songs which are inspired by the Spirit of God are powerful tools that bring messages of hope, healing and happiness directly to His people. God has given us an exhortation in Colossians 3:16 which should be heeded by each of His children. Let the word of Christ dwell in you richly, with all wisdom; teaching and admonishing one another in psalms and hymns and spiritual songs, singing with grace in your hearts to the Lord.

Throughout the centuries, God has entrusted men and women to bring Him adoration and thanksgiving through anointed music. The Bible contains a multitude of messages concerning the songs of praise to God. An example is found in Psalm 105:2, "Sing to Him, sing praises to Him; tell of all His wondrous works!"

In the vast majority of my interviews with the songwriters, the authors refused to take an ounce of credit for the birth of their songs, adding "It was like taking dictation. The song was a gift from God." Some writers declared that the song came so fast it was difficult to write it on paper. Others said, "I had no intention of writing a song at the time. It came as a wonderful surprise." Still others said, "I never intended to sing the song other than in my private devotional periods."

One fact or characteristic concerning so many of the stories behind famous hymns, as well as contemporary praise and worship songs, is that they are born out of dark and gloomy situations in the lives of the authors. Into the shadows God sends rays of "sunlight" in the form of biblical lyrics and beautiful melodies which are later shared with Christians around the world. Thus, the Scripture presented with this book: *"Until the day break, and the shadows flee away"* (Song of Solomon 2:17).

Some of these songs stories are humorous, some are very somber, some are incredibly intriguing, but all are true—true stories behind the greatest hymns and songs of praise of all time.

1

A Cold Night In Germany

A Mighty Fortress Is Our God

God is our refuge and strength, a very present help in trouble (Psalm 46:1).

The strains of "A Mighty Fortress Is Our God" could be heard drifting through the portals of the gigantic Washington National Cathedral on September 14, 2001. It was part of the National Service of Prayer and Remembrance, just three days following the 9/11 attack on America. Below is the account of how that memorable song was written.

On a cold, windy night in Germany in the early 1500s, a young peasant, Martin Luther, came very near being hit by a bolt of lighting during a thunderstorm. Following his close call with death he changed his course of study from law to theology. His education continued until he had earned a Doctorate of Philosophy degree.

Through his studies, he discovered that true Christianity did not depend upon what one knows about God, but upon a right personal relationship with God. God's forgiveness through the sacrificial death of Christ became all-important to Luther.

One day he thought, "If only I could make the pilgrimage to Rome." That dream was fulfilled, and while crawling up a staircase called Scala Sancta, on his knees, he remembered the verse of Scripture, The just shall live by faith. He sprang to his feet, ran back down the stairs, and the Reformation began.

To God Be the Glory

The greatest work that Luther accomplished was the translation of the New Testament into the language of the people. Then to the amazement of everyone, Martin Luther began to write hymns and gospel songs. The people sang them with great fervor. Luther preached long and hard, becoming a forceful leader of one of the world's greatest spiritual awakenings.

Hymnbooks began to be used in the schools and homes, as well as in the churches. Christian worship songs became a spring of spirituality in the hearts and lives of the people.

The song for which Luther will be remembered is "A Mighty Fortress Is Our God," written in about 1527. It exalts God to a high and lofty position in the minds and hearts of those who believe the message of the song. It is a paraphrase of Psalm 46.

On the base of Luther's tomb is inscribed, "A Mighty Fortress Is Our God." It is said to be the greatest hymn of the greatest man in the greatest period in German history. Historians declare that it has been sung by persecuted people on their way to exile, and by martyrs at their death. The song is rugged and strong, much like Luther himself. Frederick H. Hedge translated it from German in 1853.

A mighty fortress is our God
A bulwark never failing
Our helper He amid the flood
Of mortal ills prevailing
For still our ancient foe
Doth seek to work us woe
His craft and power are great
And armed with cruel hate
On earth is not His equal.

On March 31, 1969, this hymn was also heard at the Washington National Cathedral as part of the memorial service following the death of Dwight David Eisenhower, our 34th President.

Reflection: Every person who is a Christian should take solace in the fact that we serve a loving Heavenly Father who is a God of power and might, and who has our best interest in sharper focus than we can imagine.

2

At Churchill's Birthplace

Majesty

Who being the brightness of his glory, and the express image of his person, and upholding all things by the word of his power; when he had by himself purged our sins, sat down on the right hand of the majesty on high (Hebrews 1:3).

Dr. Jack Hayford, for many years pastor of the famed Church On The Way in Van Nuys, California, traveled to England for a seminar in Oxford. Mrs. Hayford was with him. The year was the silver anniversary of the coronation of Elizabeth II as Queen of England. Dr. Hayford reports that he was completely caught up in the emotion of the occasion. As he walked among the people and saw them move about amid signs of history on every hand, he sensed a feeling of grandeur and nobility. While touring the countryside, the Hayfords made a short visit to Blenheim Palace where Winston Churchill was born and raised and where he would occasionally go aside for a short rest during the horrors of World War II.

Memories of those days and what had gone before came rushing back to Pastor Hayford. As he looked about he sensed, too, that even though individuals are greatly used in the course of man's existence on this earth, there is a greater power, the One who is the Author of our destiny.

To God Be the Glory

Dr. Hayford realized that there was a deep feeling in the hearts of the English people for the royalty who stood with them in dark hours. Even now they were excited about sharing in the celebration of their monarch. Suddenly there came to his mind a feeling that Christ wants His church to have such a sense of loyalty and fellowship, because He must be our leader in good times and bad.

As Dr. Hayford stood on the magnificent, well-groomed landscape surrounding Blenheim Palace, he said to his wife, "Honey, I can hardly describe to you all the things which this setting evokes in me. There is something of majesty in all this, and I believe it has a great deal to do with why people who lived here have been of such consequence in the shaping of history."

As he talked to her of how Christ wants to exercise His kingdom authority in our lives and our being, one word seemed to charge to the forefront: MAJESTY! The word seemed at the moment to represent the glory, excellence, grace, and power of Christ. By comparison, Queen Elizabeth seemed but a paltry reminder of the royal heritage we enjoy as we worship the majesty of our risen Lord.

As the Hayfords drove away from Blenheim Palace, Dr. Hayford said, "Take the notebook and write down some words, will you Babe?" He then began to the lyrics and the notes to one of the most popular worship songs now being used by Christians worldwide.

The song was edited and completed some time later at the piano in the living room of their home. Never in their wildest dreams could the Hayfords have imagined the impact that this song would have on the singing of Christians in so many lands.

Reflection: When we see the great King and are face to face with His glory, it will be wonderful to forever adore His majesty and His power. While we wait, we bow to His authority as we "lift up on high the Name of Jesus."

3

A College Student's Victory

At Calvary

But he was wounded for our transgressions, he was bruised for our iniquities: the chastisement of our peace was upon him; and with his stripes we are healed (Isaiah 53:5).

Dr. Reuben A. Torrey, President of Moody Bible Institute (MBI) in Chicago, in 1905, told the following story."

While president of MBI I received a letter from a pastor, a very concerned father of a teenage son. The young man was causing himself and his family a great deal of trouble and mental anguish. His dad sensed that his son needed to be under the influence of the daily teaching of the Bible, coupled with the fellowship of Christian young people. So, in the letter he asked if his son might be enrolled at MBI.

"I answered his letter, telling him that I was running a school where future missionaries and pastors were being trained, not a reform school. This did not deter the young man's dad. He continued to plead his son's case."

Dr. Torrey, too, was a father and he could "feel" the heart of this dad who was so broken and concerned for his son. Finally, after several weeks, Dr. Torrey gave in. He contacted the dad, telling him that his son could enter MBI, but with certain stipulations and conditions. He was to faithfully attend classes, obey all of the rules and each day stop by his office. The Dad and the young man agreed, so MBI had a new student." Dr. Torrey later said, "I never saw a young man with more problems, especially in the spiritual realm."

As time went by the young man was as good as his word. He tried to be a good student, he obeyed the rules and he stopped by Dr. Torrey's office each day, if only to say "hello." As days became weeks and weeks rolled into months, little improvements were seen in the young man's life.

One day he burst into Dr. Torrey's office with his face aglow. He announced that God has saved him. The Lord had come into his life. They rejoiced together. He became a model college student, and later in his life became one of the great Bible teachers of our country. His name is William R. Newell. Newell later declared to his friend, Al Smith, "If I hadn't gone through that experience I, perhaps, would never would have come to know the importance of God's Word and the wonderful truth of salvation by grace."

Newell became a faculty member of MBI and while there wrote—in verse form—his salvation experience. He said, "As I read what I had written, I realized that it was a word picture of what had happened in my life, and it could happen in the lives of so many more people."

He showed his poem to Dr. Daniel B. Towner, head of the music department, leaving it with him. Later the two met in a hallway and Towner said, "Bill, I was so taken by the poem you gave me that I went immediately to my studio and composed a tune. I feel that it could be the best song that either of us will ever write in our lifetime." The first stanza:

Years I spent in vanity and pride,
Caring not my Lord was crucified.
Knowing not it was for me he died
At Calvary.

Reflection: The Lord let William Newell see, through the Scriptures, what He had done in his life. It is a testimony of how Christ saves us and brings us to Himself.

4

Strength for a Grieving Mother

God Will Make a Way

...I will even make a way in the wilderness and rivers in the desert (Isaiah 43:19b).

I have often reported that most of the songs that are meaningful to Christians were born during a dark period in someone's life. Into the shadows God sends a sunbeam—a song. A tragedy of epic proportions was the background for the writing of one of Don Moen's most influential and widely known songs. Following is how Don related his story to me:

"My wife's sister and her husband, Craig and Susan Phelps, were involved in a car accident during a ski trip they were taking from their home in Oklahoma to a resort in Colorado. Way out somewhere in the Texas panhandle, their van was hit by an eighteen-wheeler. As they approached a remote intersection, Craig did not see the truck coming, and the driver of the truck did not see their van. The truck hit a rear panel of the van with such force that all four of their children were thrown out.

"In the darkness only the crying of their severely injured children made it possible for mom and dad to find them—all except one—their nine-year-old son, whom they finally located lying by a nearby fence. He was already dead. His neck had been broken. Craig, a physician, knew that he could not help that child, so he spent his time trying to help the other children. They sat for forty-five minutes, out in the wilderness, waiting for an ambulance.

To God Be the Glory

"I received word of the tragedy from my mother-in-law, but I hesitated to call Craig. I had no idea what to say to him. He was a physician who deals with life and death on a daily basis, and now his own son was in his arms, dead.

"They asked me to sing at the funeral, so I boarded a plane the next day, March 19, 1987, and headed for Oklahoma. As I sat on the plane, wondering what I should say to them, I began to read in the book of Isaiah. My eyes went to chapter 43, verse 19, '...I will even make a way in the wilderness, and rivers in the desert.' Instantly, the Lord gave me a song to sing to them. I sketched it out on a legal pad.

"After the funeral, I was sitting with them, holding them in my arms. I cried with them, and through my tears I said, 'The Lord gave me a song for you.' And I began singing...

God will make a way
Where there seems to be no way
He works in ways we cannot see
He will make a way for me.

And on until he had finished the song."

Susan later related how that she made a quick decision between the time she got out of the van and the time they found her son. She knew that she had to make a choice between becoming bitter and angry and accepting God's plan for their family at that time.

Reflection: In times of trials, and especially in times of extreme trial, we need to keep the thought close to our hearts that God loves us and will provide for our every need.

5

Springing From a Novel

Jesus Loves Me This I Know

But Jesus called them unto him, and said, Suffer little children to come unto me, and forbid them not: for of such is the kingdom of God (Luke 18:16).

One of the most tender, touching and timeless songs ever written was created by two ladies who also taught some of the most courageous, confident and chivalrous soldiers ever to set foot on a battlefield. The ladies were Anna and Susan Warner, sisters, and they lived on Constitution Island near West Point Academy. Thomas Warner, the Chaplain at West Point, was their uncle. Anna and Susan taught Sunday school classes and invited the cadets to attend. Many of them accepted their invitations.

When the sisters died West Point honored their memories by allowing them to be buried in the Academy Cemetery—an unusual exception to the rules, but a high honor, indeed! I wonder if the officer who allowed it was at an earlier time a participant in their Sunday school classes.

While living near the Academy a situation arose that made it necessary that Anna and Susan help with the family income. They almost immediately turned to writing books—novels—that became best sellers of that day.

During Susan's writing of a novel, *Say and Seal*, she asked Anna if she would write a children's song of comfort to be sung by a dying child in the story. Anna responded with the lyrics to the now famous "Jesus Loves Me." Susan's book was published in 1860.

Two years later William B. Bradbury, composer of many famous Christian songs—two of which were "The Solid Rock" and "Sweet Hour of Prayer"—was moved to write a melody for Anna's simple and very meaningful song lyrics. For 152 years millions of children in many lands have sung "Jesus Loves Me."

In more contemporary times famous artists such as Whitney Houston, Bobby Womack, Kenny Loggins, Sting, Dolly Parton and Aretha Franklin have recorded it. Stories have grown up around the song. One account is that Karl Barth, the famed theologian, was asked to summarize the essence of the Christian faith in only a few words. He responded, "Jesus loves me, this I know, for the Bible tells me so." Another is that at the height of persecution in Communist China a Christian sent a message to a friend. The message escaped the attention of the censors because it simply said, "The this I know people are well." It assured the friend that the church in China was alive and well.

Jesus loves me! This I know,
For the Bible tells me so;
Little ones to Him belong,
They are weak but He is strong.
Jesus loves me! He who died,
Heaven's gate to open wide;
He will wash away my sin,
Let His little child come in.

Chorus:

Yes, Jesus loves me!
Yes, Jesus loves me!
Yes, Jesus loves me!
The Bible tells me so.

Reflection: Every man, woman, boy or girl wants to be loved. Deep within each of us there is a desire to know that someone cares for me. Jesus died for you, knowing that you might never love Him back.

6

From the Kitchen Table

The Old Rugged Cross

And He bearing His cross went forth into a place called the place of the skull, which is called in the Hebrew Galgotha: Where they crucified Him... (John19:17-18a).

When polls are taken to determine the most popular American hymns, invariably near the top of the list is "The Old Rugged Cross." It has been the most favored of the approximate three hundred songs written by George Bennard.

Bennard was born into a very modest family in Youngstown, Ohio in 1873. His father passed away during George's teen years, leaving the youth with tremendous family responsibilities. To that end he became a coal miner, as was his father before him. For a number of years, following his marriage, he and his wife worked with the Salvation Army.

George later became an itinerant Methodist preacher and served for several years in Canada and in some of our northern states. Bennard had a favorite Scripture verse, John 3:16. When quoting the verse he seemed to always have a vision of a cross—a crude Roman instrument of death. It was stained with the blood of Christ, who gave His life in order that we might become Christians.

On one occasion, as he was thinking of Christ's crucifixion, an original melody ran through his mind. He later reported that although it was a complete melody, very few words came with it. He struggled to write some appropriate lyrics, but all that came was the passage, "I'll cherish the old rugged cross." The song seemed to take shape in bits and pieces. He completed the chorus and was pleased with his efforts, but the verses he composed did not seem proper and suitable.

He returned from several preaching engagements to his home—1101 E. Michigan Avenue, Albion, Michigan—with a renewed meaning of the cross etched into his mind and heart. He took the manuscript, on which he had labored for so long, and placed it on the kitchen table. In a very short span of time he was able to rewrite the stanzas with each word falling perfectly into place. He asked his wife to join him in the kitchen. She did so and he joyfully sang his prized, new song for her to hear. She was very pleased and expressed that the song was great!

He then sent the manuscript to Charles H. Gabriel, in Chicago, asking if he would write the proper chords with the melody line. Gabriel did so and returned the song with the message, "You will hear from this song."

Bennard said what I have heard countless other songwriters say, "I really didn't write it. I was merely the instrument that God used."

A plaque, identifying a State of Michigan Historic Site, marks the location on Michigan Avenue in Albion, Michigan, where Bennard wrote the song. It reads, in part: BIRTHPLACE OF "OLD RUGGED CROSS" .... one of the world's best-loved hymns, was composed there in 1912.....

On a hill far away stood an old rugged cross,
The emblem of suff'ring and shame.
And I love that old cross where the dearest and best
For a world of lost sinners was slain.
So I'll cherish the old rugged cross,
'Till my trophies at last I lay down.
I will cling to the old rugged cross,
And exchange it some day for a crown."

George Bennard lived his retirement years in Reed City, Michigan and passed away there in 1958.

Reflection: The cross of Christ has become a badge of honor for you and me. The suffering He endured on that Roman instrument of crucifixion and death was for our eternal salvation.

7

A Teen's Experience in the Kitchen

Hallelujah, Praise the Lamb

I will bless the LORD at all times: his praise shall continually be in my mouth (Psalm 34:1).

Pam is the daughter of Bruce and Ruth Thum. She was born near San Diego, California. Bruce and Ruth traveled as an evangelistic team and often Pam traveled with them. She started singing in the meetings at a very early age. She and her mom, who played several instruments, wrote little songs together during her childhood.

Pam said, "When I was six I walked down the isle of one of my dad's services and made a public profession of my faith in Christ. Even as a child I knew that Jesus was my best Friend.

"I remember when I was in my teen years, and still traveling with mom and dad, we were staying in an apartment owned by a church, in Miami, Florida. I had traveled my entire life and I remembered that I had said goodbye to so many friends along the way—friends that I probably would never see again here on the earth. A sadness came over me that was so heavy. I was normally a happy person, but I couldn't seem to handle this weight.

"I tried to pray and it didn't seem to work. It was so overwhelming. I remember that my parents just didn't know what to do about my problem. It seemed so abnormal. When they went to sleep I was still up. I went to the kitchen and began walking around in that little space.

To God Be the Glory

"I remember hearing in my mind the words of David that I had read in the Psalms, 'I will bless the Lord at all times: His praise shall continually be in my mouth.' It took all my strength to just talk out loud, but I began to say, 'I love you Jesus.' Then I began to sing it. It was so hard to sing. As I was singing various phrases to the Lord, suddenly out of my mouth came 'hallelujah! praise the Lamb' and on an on through what is now a praise chorus. The melody came with it.

"I then felt the weight lifting off of me. The heaviness left. I felt joy and strength stirring in me again. I sang that chorus again and again; it must have been for two hours. I was laughing and crying and dancing around the kitchen. The presence of God seemed to dispel all of the sadness. Strength and joy was back again! The following morning my parents had me to share that chorus with the church and they responded so joyfully.

"I recorded 'Hallelujah, Praise the Lamb,' and so did the Talleys—Roger, Debra and Kirk. The Brooklyn Tabernacle Choir also put it on one of their albums. Those recordings helped to spread the song around the U.S. It was later sung by the thousand-voice choir of the Billy Graham Crusades, with the congregation joining in on a repeat of the chorus."

During these times church congregations, worship gatherings, and revival campaigns universally sing this praise chorus.

Reflection: As this song suggests, try singing to the Lord with your whole heart, not just with your voice—singing and making melody in your heart to the Lord (Ephesians 5:19).

8

I Have a Jewel

Blessed Assurance

Every day will I bless thee; and I will praise thy name forever and ever (Psalm 145:2).

Fanny Crosby, America's most prolific hymn writer, wrote 8,000 Gospel songs and hymns during a lifetime that spanned nearly a century. She passed away in her ninety-fifth year. All of her days, except the first six weeks, were spent in blindness. However, not even the loss of eyesight could render defeat to this astoundingly courageous soul. Aunt Fanny, as she later was affectionately called, also wrote 1,000+ nonreligious songs, and had four books of poetry and two best-selling autobiographies published.

Frances Jane Crosby was born in Putnam County, New York, on March 24, 1820. A poorly trained doctor applied a mustard plaster poultice to her eyes when she was only six weeks old, rendering her totally blind. Even in her childhood she realized she had a special gift. She often said, "I have a jewel—content." When only nine years of age she wrote:

O what a happy soul am I,
Although I cannot see,
I am resolved that in this world
Contented I will be.
How many blessings I enjoy
That other people don't.
To weep and sigh because I'm blind,
I cannot and I won't.

To God Be the Glory

During her fifteenth year she entered the New York Institute for the Blind. Her record there was such that after graduation she was asked to teach at the Institute. She remained on the faculty for eleven years.

She told S. Trevena Jackson her little "love story," which he recorded in his book, *Fanny Crosby's Story of Ninety-Four Years*, She said:

"Some people seem to forget that blind girls have just as great a faculty for loving, and do love just as much and just as truly as those who have their sight. When I was about twenty a gifted young man by the name of Alexander Van Alstyne came to our Institute. He was also blind and a musician. We soon became very much concerned for each other.... I placed my right hand on his left and called him 'Van.' From that hour two lives looked on a new universe, for love met love, and all the world was changed. On March the fifth in the year 1858 we were united in marriage. I became a mother and knew a mother's love, but the angels came down and took our infant up to God.

"One day in 1873, Aunt Fanny was visiting with a friend, Mrs. Joseph Knapp, a musician of sorts and wife of the founder of Metropolitan Life Insurance Company. During their visit Mrs. Knapp played a tune on her piano that she had recently written. She then asked Fanny, 'What does this tune say?' After kneeling in prayer for a few moments, she rose and declared, 'It says, "Blessed assurance, Jesus is mine!"" Aunt Fanny began to dictate verses to Mrs. Knapp, who wrote them down, fitting them to the melody just as we hear it sung today."

Blessed assurance, Jesus is mine!
O what a foretaste of glory divine!
Heir of salvation, purchase of God.
Born of His Spirit, washed in His blood.

Chorus:
This is my story, this is my song,
Praising my Savior, all the day long,
This is my story, this is my song,
Praising my Savior, all the day long.

Fanny Crosby died February 12, 1915.

Reflection: No song is more meaningful than one that declares our relationship to the Heavenly Father and is at the same time a song of praise to Him.

9

Singing with "Condi" Rice

His Eye Is On the Sparrow

Are not two sparrows sold for a farthing? and one of them shall not fall on the ground without your Father...Fear ye not therefore, ye are of more value than many sparrows (Matthew 10:29, 31).

The scene is a hotel suite in Jacksonville, Florida. It is midnight on New Years even, 2002, and a group of friends of Condoleezza Rice have gathered in her room following the Gator Bowl® football game and a late dinner. During their time of fellowship and converation, they joined hands and hearts and prayed for the world and the future. Then they all sang "His Eye Is on the Sparrow," a song made famous in the mid 1900s by another prominent black lady, Ethel Waters.

It is indeed significant that the world's most powerful woman, raised in a pastor's home in Birmingham, Alabama, recognizes that Jesus Christ watches each of us—His children. Miss Rice, now Secretary of State, has a close friend who remarked, "Her faith is absolutely fundamental to who she is. It is part of her fiber." She also had a grandmother who would always say to her as she was leaving the house, "Take the name of Jesus with you."

The message of the inspiring song being sung on New Year's eve had an unusual birth. Mrs. Civilla D. Martin, a Canadian, after her education in the schools of Nova Scotia became a school teacher. Before long she had met and married Dr. William Martin, an evangelist and musician of sorts, and joined him in his itinerant work.

To God Be the Glory

Early into the 1900s Mrs. Martin heard of a dear friend who had been overtaken with a severe state of depression. She became quite burdened for her friend and made her way by train to see the lady who lived in Elmira, New York.

While there Mrs. Martin told her friend of an incident which happened a short time earlier, when she experienced God protecting hand during an illness. She hoped that the story would be an encouragement to the depressed soul.

After hearing the story her friend said, "You know, I shouldn't worry, should I? We are promised in the Bible that God watches over the little sparrows." Mrs. Martin agreed, "He surely does."

When she arrived back home, she sat down and penned the words to one of the most beautiful and famous of all the gospel songs, "His Eye Is On the Sparrow." Charles H. Gabriel wrote the music.

Why should I feel discouraged,
Why should the shadows come,
Why should my heart be lonely,
And long for heaven and home?
When Jesus is my portion,
My constant Friend is He,
His eye is on the sparrow,
And I know He watches me.

Chorus:
I sing because I'm happy.
I sing because I'm free,
For His eye is on the sparrow,
And I know He watches me.

Since Condoleezza Rice's days as Provost of Stanford University, two of her favorite songs have been, "I Need Thee Every Hour" and "His Eye Is on the Sparrow."

Reflection: None of us would ever fret or worry over a single problem if we could gain a deep-seated assurance that our Heavenly Father really cares for us. He cares more for me than I am able to care for myself.

10

A Pastor Gets Heated Up

He Lives

He is not here, for He is risen, as He said. Come, see the place where the Lord lay (Matthew 28:6).

"It's a lie!!" shouted Pastor Alfred H. Ackley one Easter Sunday morning in 1932, as he was getting ready to preach in his church in Escondido, California. He was listening to the radio while shaving with a straight razor. His outburst came because he heard someone on the air say, "Good morning folks, it's Easter! You know, folks, it really doesn't make any difference to me if Christ be risen or not. As far and I am concerned His body could be as dust in some Palestinian tomb. The main thing is, His truth goes marching on!"

The whole matter seemed to ignite a blaze under Ackley, even with his razor in his hand. He believed, with all of his being, the Biblical accounts that Christ had risen from the tomb, bodily. His wife heard him shouting and asked, "Why are you yelling so early in the morning?" Ackley said, "Didn't you hear what that man said? He said that it didn't matter whether Christ had risen, bodily, or not!"

Well, that morning Ackley preached as he had never preached before. He could not set aside the fact that someone, on the radio, would utter such sacrilege. After Ackley and his wife had gotten home from church, she could see that he was still fretting over the situation. She did something that has had lasting results. She told her husband, "Listen here Alfred Ackley, it's time for you to do what you do best. Then you will have something that will go on telling the story." He got the message and went to his piano and began to compose a song. When he had finished the tremendously popular "He Lives" had been born.

I serve a risen Saviour, He's in the world today;
I know that He is living, Whatever men may say;
I see His hand of mercy, I hear His voice of cheer,
And just the time I need Him He's always near.

Chorus:
He lives, He lives,
Christ Jesus lives today!
He walks with me and He talks with me
Along life's narrow way.
He lives, He lives, salvation to impart!
You ask me how I know He lives:
He lives within my heart.

Alfred Ackley was born on January 21, 1887, in Spring Hill, Pennsylvania. He received a thorough education in music, including study in composition at the Royal Academy of Music in London, England. As a performer, he was recognized as an accomplished cellist.

Following graduation from the Westminster Theological Seminary, in 1914, he was ordained to the Presbyterian ministry. He always maintained a keen interest in the writing of hymns and Gospel songs. It is estimated that he wrote well over 1,000 songs and hymns in addition to aiding in the compilation of various hymnals and songbooks. In recognition of his contribution to sacred music, he was awarded an honorary Doctorate of Sacred Music Degree from John Brown University. Dr. Ackley died in Whittier, California, on July 3, 1960.

Of all the Atkley accomplishments mentioned in this column, none was greater than the writing of the notable "He Lives!"

Reflection: The resurrection of Christ is the doctrine in the Bible that supports all other claims made by our wonderful Savior.

11

Victory Follows His Prayer

Hallelujah Chorus

Of the increase of His government and peace there shall be no end... (Isaiah 9:7).

"MUSIC! Where is it coming from?" asked George Handel as he and his wife, Dorothea, quickly sat up in bed. It was the middle of the night and they could hear music in the house. After a thorough search of their home they could not find the source of it. As a last resort they decided to go to the attic where their son slept. There, sitting on his bed, they found him playing a clavier, a small keyboard instrument. His uncle, who knew young George loved music, had secretly given it to him.

Handel was born February 24, 1685, in Halle, Germany, to a family of no musical distinction. However, his own musical talent manifested itself so clearly that before his tenth birthday he began to receive from a local organist his only formal musical instructions. Handel's mother, the daughter of a Lutheran preacher, made sure of his early spiritual training. However, his father, a surgeon, insisted that he study law. He was able to continue his music career after his father's death, which occurred while he was still in college.

Handel's first job was as a church organist, beginning just after his seventeenth birthday. His musical preference lay elsewhere. By age nineteen he had mastered most of the orchestral instruments.

To God Be the Glory

He received wide recognition as a music composer in Italy and Germany; however, his greatest fame sprang from a concert in Ireland. In Dublin on April 13, 1742, at Neal's Music Hall, a choir rises and "Hallelujah! Hallelujah! Hallelujah! Hallelujah!" fills the auditorium. A great crowd had gathered to hear the premiere of what was destined to become the most widely known musical in the world, Handel's *Messiah*.

King George II of England was in attendance. He was so moved by the exhilarating music he sprang to his feet, an action that seemed to prompt the whole audience to do the same. From that day, wherever in the world the "Hallelujah Chorus" is presented, the audience stands.

Handel found fame and fortune in England, especially among royalty and noblemen. While continuing his musical adventures, he became one of the leading composers in the world.

In his fifty-seventh year Handel determined to write something that would be lasting and would lift the spirits of all who heard. Following an extended season of prayer he took a series of Scriptures, compiled and arranged by Charles Jennens, and began his task. Twenty-three days later he rose from his labors a victor. He had written his immortal *Messiah*, an oratorio that has become the most widely performed musical in the world. Every year thousands of performances of the *Messiah* are heard during the Christmas holiday season, especially the "Hallelujah Chorus."

In the hours just before his death Handel said, "I want to die in the hope of rejoining the good God, my sweet Lord and Savior on the day of His resurrection." Included in the lyrics of the *Messiah* are these words, "And He shall reign forever and ever, HALLELUJAH! King of kings and Lord of lords, FOREVER!"

Reflection: Each of us—in our own hearts—should offer our "hallelujahs," our exclamations of praise to God, at times in our lives when we feel His wonderful, mighty presence.

12

God Reveals His Wondrous Works

How Great Thou Art

O Lord, how great are thy works! and thy thoughts are very deep (Psalm 92:5).

During the Billy Graham Crusade in New York City in 1957 the great Crusade Choir, sang "How Great Thou Art" more than 100 consecutive times during those evangelistic services.

I have learned about the writing of the song through extensive research and from a long-time friend, Victor Nischick, who visited in the home of the English missionary who brought the song to the English-speaking world.

The life of this great hymn began in 1886 on an estate in southern Sweden, and was known in several countries before it finally reached the shores of the United States. A member of the Swedish parliament and a successful editor, walked across the beautiful grounds of the coastal estate, and during his walk was caught in a thunderstorm. He was in awe as he watched the sky go from gray to black, and then to a beautiful blue again.

In 1931 English missionary Stuart Hine first heard the song in the Russian language. He and his wife had gone to Russia as missionaries. There, they heard this very meaningful hymn that happened to be a Russian translation of Carl Boberg's Swedish song.

To God Be the Glory

Hine found himself one day in a thunderstorm as he strolled through the Carpathian Mountains with group of young people. While the lightning flashed and the thunder rolled through the mountain range, his mind went to the Russian hymn that he had heard and that had become so dear to him. English verses began to form in his mind, verses that were suggested by portions of the Russian translation.

Hine wrote a book, *Not You, But God*, which presents two additional, optional verses that he copyrighted in 1953, as a translation of the Russian version. Dr. J. Edwin Orr introduced Hine's "How Great Thou Art" in the United States in 1954. Three years later, it began its orbit around the world by way of the Billy Graham New York Crusade.

In my possession is a prized copy of "How Great Thou Art" in the Russian language. All four of the men who helped bring us this song—Boberg, the Swede, Von Glehn, the German, Prokhanoff, the Russian, and Hine the Englishman—carefully preserved the awesome message of the song. I personally held a letter in my hand from Hine's daughter, Sonia, dated March 16, 1989, which contained the somber news that Stuart Hine had died peacefully in his sleep two days before. He was ninety-two years of age. His memorial service was held at the Gospel Hall on Martello Road, Walton-on-Naze, Essex, England, on March 23, at two o'clock in the afternoon.

Reflection: God's majestic creations all testify to His omnipotence and His omniscience. As we look around us, on the things He has made, we, too, stand in awe of the Creator, the Power of all the universe. And just think...this great God has chosen to live in my heart, and yours, and all who have accepted His gift of love, and have made Christ the Lord in their lives.

13

Out of Darkness, a Sunbeam

Because He Lives

Yet a little while, and the world seeth me no more; but ye see me: because I live, ye shall live also (John 14:19).

I dare say that there is not a Southern Gospel Music fan on the face of the earth who has not heard a song written by Bill and Gloria Gaither. More and more millions of Americans and people of other countries are now coming to love Southern Gospel, and most of them can name more than one Gaither song. The Gaither Homecoming concerts and videos are the primary purpose. One of the best known of the songs of Bill and Gloria Gaither is the subject of this story.

When both were single and teaching in the same high school they met and began to share ideas about songs. Gloria, the English major in college, would become in later years the predominant writter of the lyrics in their songs, while Bill's forte was the musical setting. Bill had also earned a Master's degree that allowed him to become the head of the English department of their high school. The joint efforts, that had its beginning in that school, blossomed into the most prolific husband and wife songwriting team of modern times.

Bill and Gloria wrote their first song together several decades ago. Their songs, almost without fail start with an idea. Bill, on most occasions, would write a music setting with an idea in mind and then Gloria, using the same idea would write the words. Gloria revealed in her book, "Because He Lives," that on some occasions the whole lyric would come to her, to which Bill alone or with a co-writer would write the music. They have now written some 600 songs, produced sixty recordings and several musicals. Both are authors or co-authors of several books.

To God Be the Glory

Now for the story behind "Because He Lives." In the late 1960s, while expecting their third child, the Gaithers were going through a rather traumatic time in their lives. Bill was recovering from a bout with mononucleosis. They and other members in their church family were the objects of false accusations and belittlement. It was a special time of fear and torment for Gloria. The thought of bringing another child into this world with all of the craziness, was taking its toll on her.

She remembers that on New Year's Eve she was sitting in their living room, in agony and fear. The educational system was being infiltrated with the "God is dead" idea, while drug abuse and racial tension were increasing. Then suddenly and quite unexpectedly, she was filled with a sweet, calming peace. It was as if her Heavenly Father, like an attentive mother bending over her baby, saw His Gloria and came to her rescue. The panic gave way to a calmness and an assurance that only the Lord can give. She was assured that the future would be just fine, left in God's hands.

Both Bill and Gloria remembered that the power of the blessed Holy Spirit seem to come to their aide. Christ's resurrection, in all of its power, was reaffirmed in their lives and their thinking. To Gloria it was "Life conquering death" in their daily lives. Joy once again dominated the fearful circumstances of the day.

All of this gave rise to one of the most famous Southern Gospel songs of our time, "Because He Lives." The first verse is a presentation of the Gospel of Christ, reminding us of His death, burial and resurrection. In the second verse we see the life of a new baby and sense the assurance that Christ alone can give. The little one can have a victorious life, because Christ lives.

We can face tomorrow, with all of the uncertainty that it brings, as we realize that God holds the future and makes life worth living for all who trust in Him.

Reflection: As we remember Christ's resurrection we gain assurance and strength to overcome the frightening obstacles of life. It is also very meaningful and empowering to realize that Jesus lives, every single day, in our hearts.

14

Lord, Is That OK?

Jesus, Name Above All Names

Wherefore God also hath highly exalted Him, and given Him a name which is above every name (Philippians 2:9).

Naida Hearn was born in Palmerston North, a peaceful town in the north of New Zealand, in 1931. She grew up learning the things of the Lord in that quiet, island nation. As she was nearing her fortieth birthday she wrote a beautiful song that has circled our globe, influencing Christians in thousands of cities and hamlets.

As she studied the Bible she became fascinated with the many different names referring to Jesus. So great was her interest that she began to make a list of the names of Christ on a sheet of paper.

As is the case with many homes in Palmerston North, she and her family had a "washhouse" behind the regular living quarters of the home. One day in the early 1970s, she made her way to the washhouse carrying with her the paper on which she had written the names of Jesus. She placed the sheet on the window seal, against the window. The paper was in full view as the did the washing. Feeling in a very worshipful mood, she suddenly found herself singing. She expressed it to me as follows:

To God Be the Glory

"While I was doing the washing the Lord just gave me the first line, 'Jesus, name above all names,' to sing. I just started it and carried on singing. I sang the whole song just as you sing it today. I just opened my mouth and all of the words came out, the pitch and everything. I just sang."

She continued, "I thought, 'Well, I'll write it down.' The Lord said, 'Yes,' so I left the washing and went down into the sitting room and found a key that was just right, and worked it out on manuscript paper."

Jesus, name above all names
Beautiful Savior, glorious Lord.
Emmanuel, God is with us.
Blessed Redeemer, Living word.

"I said, 'Lord, is that OK? Is it all right like that? Yes, it was all right. That was all I wrote, and then I went back to the washing. It was just that simple. It was a straight-out lead from the Holy Spirit, absolutely."

Soon thereafter it was sung in her church, New Life Church in Palmerton North. She didn't remember who sang it, but I can guess that it was she who presented it to her congregation. She had a beautiful singing voice. She sang it for me on the phone, and I prize the tape on which I recorded it. It is surprisingly clear and good, even by long distance from New Zealand.

Visitors from other parts of her country, who attended the church service, took the song to their churches. Missionaries began to carry it overseas where it quickly became a favorite. Soon it was being sung in several nations. Jesus, Name Above All Names, continues to be one of the most popular praise choruses in the world today.

Naida told me her story in 1999. I had another visit by phone with her in April, 2001. In that same month, as I interviewed another songwriter from New Zealand, I was surprised to hear his report that she had passed away just one week earlier.

Reflection: As you consider the names given to our Savior, you, too, will be drawn closer to Him.

15

Rushing the Printer

Precious Lord, Take My Hand

I the Lord thy God will hold thy right hand... (Isaiah 41:13a).

On July 1, 1899, little notice was taken of a baby boy of color, born in Villa Rica, Georgia, a small town some forty miles west of Atlanta. He, one of seven brothers and sisters, was around the church most of his early life. His dad was a devout Baptist preacher and his mother was an organist. She started young Thomas on the piano when he was seven years old.

In his late teens he decided to embark on a career as a blues musician, billed as Georgia Tom. This took him through the night clubs of Atlanta to the jazz houses on the south side of Chicago. Because of his heritage, he very shortly tired of that kind of life and gravitated toward Christian music.

At age 21, he joined the Pilgrim Baptist Church in Chicago, where he directed choirs and wrote more than 300 songs. In a taped interview in 1977, Thomas A. Dorsey told this writer the following story, which happened forty-five years earlier:

"My wife, Nettie, was about to bear our first child. I was called to St. Louis to sing in a revival. I wondered if I should go, because of my wife's condition. She persuaded me that I should go ahead, so I, alone in my Model A, drove to St. Louis.

To God Be the Glory

"During the first night of the meetings, a lad brought a telegram to me while I was still on the platform. It was horrible news. It was a message that my wife had died giving birth to our son.

"I rushed to a phone while the people were still singing, and found that the message was true. Mr. Gus Evans drove me back to Chicago that night.

"When I arrived I found that the wonderful baby boy was seemingly fine, and yet, that night he also died. I buried my wife and little son in the same casket.

"I became very despondent and filled with grief. A few days later I visited with my good friend, Professor Frye. We walked around the campus of Annie Malone's Poro College for awhile, and then went into one of the music rooms.

"I sat down at a piano and began to improvise on the keyboard. Suddenly I found myself playing a particular melody that I hadn't played before that time. (It was an adaptation of George N. Allen's melody used with the old hymn, 'Must Jesus Bear the Cross Alone?') As I played I began to say, 'Blessed Lord, blessed Lord, blessed Lord.' My friend walked over to me and said, 'Why don't you make that precious Lord?' I then began to sing,

Precious Lord, take my hand
Lead me on, let me stand
I'm tired, I'm weak, I'm worn
Through the storm, through the night
Lead me on to the light
Take my hand, precious Lord
Lead me home

"When I finished the song we began to use it and it has been going ever since. I have gotten letters from people all over the world. It was a great tragedy, but we got the message to the world."

The song has been translated into more than thirty languages. I kept phone contact with the Dorseys until shortly before he went to heaven on January 25, 1993.

Reflection: Our lives, every day, should reflect that the good things of God are alive in us.

16

A Soon Forgotten Prophecy

The Midnight Cry

And at midnight there was a cry made, Behold the bridegroom cometh; go ye out to meet him.....watch therefore, for ye know neither the day nor the hour wherein the Son of man cometh (Matthew 25:5, 13).

"When I was seven years old a visiting preacher at our church, just before the benediction, called me out of the audience and down to the front. I was timid and hesitated, but my mother encouraged me, so I obeyed the preacher. He said to me, 'Son, this may not mean anything to you now, but one day when you are older, God will give you songs that will change lives. God told me to tell you that you will write songs.' I took that as a seven-year-old would. I forgot it." That story was told to me by Greg Day in the first part of an interview with him in 2001.

Greg was born in 1962, five years after his brother Chuck. Their parents, Bob and Grace Day, taught them to play musical instruments at an early age, Greg the piano and Chuck the guitar. Greg also played drums. Both became accomplished musicians.

By age twenty-three Greg had become an alcoholic. God began to deal with his heart, and one night, after hours of drinking, in Columbus, Georgia, at 1:30 AM, Greg finally gave in to the conviction of the Holy Spirit and went with Chuck to see the preacher who lived down the road. Chuck had been saved from a life of alcoholism and dope, just one month earlier. Greg told me, "We woke the preacher up and he led me in a simple sinners prayer. Jesus delivered me at that moment -- instantly." God saved him and immediately freed him from his alcohol addition, just as He had delivered Chuck a month earlier. Both—delivered instantly! Greg told me the following unusual story:

To God Be the Glory

"My brother and I were visiting at our parents home in Adel, Georgia. Their church was beginning a revival on Sunday morning, with a visiting evangelist, Billy Swain, as the preacher for the series of meetings. He had fasted for forty days, preparing himself for the revival. During the fast he had asked God to give him a series of messages on the Second Coming of Christ. On that first Sunday morning of the campaign he preached the first of his series of sermons called, 'The Midnight Cry.' His text was taken from Matthew, chapter 25.

"Chuck took a business card from his wallet and wrote on it, 'Midnight Cry.' He said to me, 'There is something there.' We continued to listen with interest to the preacher's sermon.

"That afternoon, after lunch with our parents, Chuck and I walked into the living room, and I sat down at the piano. Chuck said, 'You know, we could probably write a song about that sermon—about the midnight cry.' I began to play a few chords on the piano. All of a sudden I said, 'I hear the sound of a mighty rushing wind,' and Chuck answered, 'And it's closer now than it's ever been.' Then immediately I came out with, 'I can almost hear the trumpet as Gabriel sounds the call.' Chuck came right back with, 'At the midnight cry we'll be going home.' It was line upon line. I would write a line and he would write a line. That is exactly how 'Midnight Cry' was written—in about thirty minutes, total.

"That night, at the church, Chuck and I sang the song for the first time. We hadn't been singing together so it was a little rough, but the crowd seemed to be very moved with the presentation of it."

A copy of the song was sent to a touring group, Gold City, in Alabama. After listening to the tape, Gold City called the Days saying, "We like 'Midnight Cry' and would like to record it." Gold City record the song in 1987, with Ivan Parker singing the lead, and sent it out as a "single." It hit the charts with such force that it quickly went to #1. The revival preacher asked God to give him a message that would go around the world, telling people of Christ's return. God has done that through Midnight Cry. It has been used or recorded thousands of times, and is probably sung every day of the week, somewhere in the world. It was even used in the "Left Behind" movie and video.

Reflection: We often hear of the Second Coming of Christ. May the truth of His "coming in the clouds" never become common place to us. It could happen any day—at morning, noon, or at midnight. You know, it will happen at "midnight"—somewhere in the world.

17

Wonderful Displays of Care

Great Is Thy Faithfulness

It is of the Lord's mercies that we are not consumed because his compassions fail not. They are new every morning: great is thy faithfulness (Lamentations 3:22, 23).

Thomas Obediah Chisholm was born in a log cabin in Franklin, Kentucky in 1866. He received his education in a little country schoolhouse, and at age sixteen began teaching at the same school. He became a Christian at age twenty-seven, and with no college or seminary training was ordained to the Methodist ministry at age thirty-six. He served as a Methodist minister for a year, but ill health made it impossible for him to continue.

He moved to Vineland, New Jersey, where he opened an insurance office. Chisholm wrote hundreds of poems during his lifetime. In 1923 he was inspired by Lamentations 3:22, 23 to write the text for the hymn, "Great Is Thy Faithfulness."

He suffered ill health most of his adult life and therefore had a smaller than average income. Of this circumstance he said, "God has given me many wonderful displays of His providing care which have filled me with astonishing gratefulness."

To God Be the Glory

Chisholm sent the words to one of his poems, "Great Is Thy Faithfulness" to his friend, William Runyan, and Runyan wrote a musical setting. Runyan was born in 1870, in Marion, New York. As a youth, he served as a church organist. Runyan was ordained as a Methodist minister at age twenty-one and then pastored various congregations in Kansas.

Runyan was a friend of Dr. Will Houghton, the president of Moody Bible Institute, and Great Is Thy Faithfulness soon became Houghton's favorite. He invited George Beverly Shea, an unknown singer at the time, to sing hymns on the Institute's radio station. Shea, of course, included Dr. Houghton's favorite hymn in his repertoire.

Great is Thy faithfulness, O God my Father,
There is no shadow of turning with Thee;
Thou changest not, Thy compassions, they fail not,
As Thou hast been Thou forever wilt be.
Great is Thy faithfulness! Great is Thy faithfulness!
Morning by morning new mercies I see;
All I have needed Thy hand hath provided
Great is Thy faithfulness, Lord, unto me!

Through those radio broadcasts Billy Graham, then a student at Wheaton College, became familiar with George Beverly Shea and the song, "Great Is Thy Faithfulness." Graham asked Shea to become part of his ministry of evangelism. It was through their crusades that this hymn became internationally popular.

Even though he suffered ill health for most of his adult life, Chisholm lived to the ripe old age of ninety-four and wrote more than twelve hundred poems. During his later years, he lived in Ocean Grove, New Jersey, a Methodist camp meeting town, where he passed away in 1960.

Reflection: Only when we remember the faithfulness of our Savior to us, do we begin to live a victorious life in Him.

18

His Life's Work and Mission

Faith of Our Fathers

Blessed is the nation whose God is the LORD... (Psalm 33:12).

Let us be reminded that many of the American heroes who went before us had great faith in Almighty God. Some of them paid inordinate, personal prices as they would cling to and preserve their Christian heritage and traditions.

Keep in mind, also, that the foundational stronghold to which our forefathers would cling was founded in the Bible, and it was to them as dear as life itself. Much more could be told about our ancestors and the persecutions they endured during their quest for a "new land," where they could enjoy Christian freedom.

The faith of our fathers, referred to in this hymn, is their abundant trust in a loving, Heavenly Father whom they had learned about in the Scriptures—lessons that presently guide our feet each day and which make it easier to fall asleep at night.

Fredrick W. Faber made it his life's work and mission to write hymns that he thought would be helpful to his fellow Christians. He wrote approximately 150 such hymns before his death. In the opinion of this writer his crowning achievement was "Faith of Our Fathers."

The message of the song, normally found in our hymnals, is very useful in evangelical worship.

To God Be the Glory

Faith of our fathers, living still,
In spite of dungeon, fire and sword;
O how our hearts beat high with joy
Whenever we hear that glorious Word

Refrain
Faith of our fathers, holy faith!
We will be true to Thee 'til death.

As we pass through these days of remembering our "fathers"—those who have gone on before us—and the price that many of them paid for our freedom, may we remember that it is sometimes difficult to "do right" and to stand for truth and justice. You and I should be able to muster-up the tenacity required to meet our just obligations and to refrain from those things that destroy and divide—even if the stars fall.

Henri Hemy, an esteemed organist and composer, born in England on November 12, 1818, wrote the musical setting for "Faith of Our Fathers." The composition was originally written in honor of Catherine of Alexander, a fourth century lady who was put death because of her faith.

Among the great examples of the FATHERS of our nation, who stood for right in this country, are:

- George Washington, who said, "It is impossible to rightly govern the world without God and the Bible."
- John Hancock informed us that, "We recognize no sovereign but God, and no King but Jesus!"
- Then there was Frances Scott Key, the composer of our national anthem, who assured us that, "The patriot who feels himself in the service of God, and who acknowledges Him in all his ways, has the promise of Almighty direction..."
- Abraham Lincoln reminded us that, "My concern is not whether God is on our side; my greatest concern is to be on God's side. For God is always right."

Reflection: One of the greatest things experienced by Americans is the fact that our nation was built on the blood, sweat and tears of men who were faithful, beyond explanation, to the building of a nation based on Biblical principles.

19

The Cabinet Maker's Song

The Solid Rock

Therefore whosoever heareth these sayings of mine, and doeth them, I will liken him unto a wise man, which built his house upon a rock (Matthew 7:24).

Edward Mote wrote only one song, but a great song it is, indeed. It has been a favorite of Christians around the world.

Mote rose from an unruly childhood to become a great writer and preacher. He said of his youth, "My Sundays were spent on the streets (of London) in play. So ignorant was I that I did not know there was a God." As he grew older he attended Tottenham Court Road Chapel where he heard sermons by the noted John Hyatt. He soon learned from Hyatt's sermons that Jesus Christ could take away all the fears of life and give him the peace of heart and mind that he had long desired.

He became a carpenter apprentice and through hard labor and conscientious efforts came to own his own cabinet shop. One day while walking to his work he began thinking that he should write a hymn. Before he reached his shop he had the chorus, "On Christ the solid rock I stand. All other ground is sinking sand." Before the day ended he had four stanzas.

The following Sunday he visited in the home of a friend, a minister, whose wife was at the point of death. During the afternoon they read from the Scriptures and prayed with her. As the preacher looked for a hymnal to sing from, as was his custom, he could find none. Mr. Mote reached into his pocket and pulled out his verses and asked if they might be sung to her. And so they did. She seemed to enjoy them very much. Mote was so pleased that she found comfort in his verses, he had one thousand copies printed for distribution among his friends.

Sometime later Edward Mote became a Baptist preacher. His efforts made it possible for a house of worship to be built for his congregation. They were so grateful they offered to deed the property to him, but he replied, "I do not want the Chapel, I want only the pulpit; and when I cease to preach Christ, then turn me out of that."

He served this congregation for more than twenty years, never missing a single Sunday for any cause.

In his seventy-seventh year, as he lay on his bed of sickness he replied, "I think I am going to heaven—yes, I am nearing port. The truths I have preached I am now living upon, and they will do to die upon. Ah! The precious blood which takes away all our sins. It is this which makes peace with God."

What a victorious ending of a useful life. He was reared in a godless home, learned an honorable trade and gave it all up to become a preacher. His memory will remain for generations because he took time one day to write:

My hope is built on nothing less
Than Jesus' blood and righteousness.
I dare not trust the sweetest frame,
But wholly lean on Jesus' name.

Chorus:
On Christ the solid Rock, I stand;
All other ground is sinking sand,
All other ground is sinking sand.

Reflection: God needs men and women who are willing to serve Him in whatever capacity or situation He may place them. It is our solemn duty as sincere Christians to rest on the "Solid Rock" and be obedient Christians. The message of the song, normally found in our hymnals, is very useful in evangelical worship.

20

A Broken Fast Gives Place to a Song

More Precious Than Silver

In whom [Christ] are hid all the treasures of wisdom and knowledge (Colossians 2:3).

Lynn DeShazzo, was born to Thomas and Bettie DeShazo in Birmingham, Alabama in 1956. She developed a love for music at an early age, learning to play the guitar by age eleven. In her teen years she wanted desperately to improve her music ability and tried to do so by playing her guitar along with songs she heard on the radio.

In her first year at Auburn University, Auburn, Alabama, she developed a desire to write Christian songs—songs that would be expressions of her heart to the Lord and that would be meaningful to people who heard them.

After graduation, in 1978, with a degree in recreation administration, she took a job at McDonald's®—not the most likely place for an Auburn alumni to work—yet, it provided for her livelihood during the first months following graduation. She also learned very valuable spiritual lessons as she continued her involvement with a campus church at Auburn called Maranatha Ministries. One such lesson was "fasting," as taught in the Scriptures.

To God Be the Glory

One Wednesday she found herself in a precarious situation. Her boss at McDonald's® had assigned her to "fry duty," the task of cooking the french fries. It just happened to be a day of "fasting" for her. Well, needless to say, the battle was on!

She related to me in an interview that the fries smelled oh, so good!! As the day wore on her hunger became more extreme . After looking around to make sure that no one would see her, she slipped a few fries into her mouth. At that moment she was almost overcome with guilt—guilt that she declared to me was "two-fold." She knew that she had broken her "fast" and that she had done it with stolen french fries.

After work that day, and as soon as she could get alone with the Lord, she earnestly asked His forgiveness for breaking her fast and for taking something that did not belong to her. She was led to Colossians, chapter 2, and particularly to verse 7, where she found that in Christ are the hidden "treasures of wisdom and knowledge." She also went to Proverbs chapter 8, which reveals that there arespiritual things that are more precious than silver and gold or precious jewels, and that nothing we desire compares with our Lord.

She had her guitar with her and as she began to play the Lord dropped a song into her heart—like a day spring from on high. The first words that came into her heart were Lord you are more precious than silver. The second line followed as easily: Lord you are more costly than gold. And on and on until the song was finished with the words: "Nothing I desire compares with Thee."

At that moment she felt so blessed. As the guilt had been two-fold, so too was the blessing. She was overtaken with the joy of God's forgiveness and the excitement of His gift—a beautiful song, "More Precious Than Silver."

It has since been translated into several languages and continues to be sung in other counties as well as in the United States. It ranks very high on the list of popular praise choruses.

Reflection: When things seem to be going a bit sideways, examine yourself to see if the greatest longing of your heart compares with the One written about in this song.

21

Born In a Dark Room

In the Garden

...he shewed unto them his hands and his side. Then were the disciples glad, when they saw the Lord (John 20:20).

"He looked a little like a southern colonel with his white mustache and a small flower in his lapel. His extraordinary sense of humor and dry wit could be very caustic if he thought the occasion demanded it—a truly brilliant man." This is a description of C. Austin Miles, the man who wrote the song which is the subject of this story. Its popularity is enormous and prolonged.

According to some polls "In the Garden" is popular abroad, as well as in the United States. More than a million recordings and printed copies of it have been sold. It is virtually impossible to pick up a standard hymnal and find it omitted.

Miles attended the Philadelphia College of Pharmacy and the University of Pennsylvania. In 1892 he abandoned his career as a pharmacist and wrote his first Gospel song, which was published by the Hall-Mack Company. He later became editor and manager of the music publishing company, and served them for thirty-seven years. He said of himself, "It is as a writer of gospel songs I am proud to be known, for in that way I may be of the most use to my Master, whom I serve willingly although not as efficiently as is my desire."

Miles' hobby was photography and he had managed to build his own "darkroom" for developing his film. He discovered one day that he could read his Bible in the special "red lighting" of the darkroom. He often read passages of Scripture as he waited for the developing process to finish. Since he was a musician and a songwriter he often found himself reading with the express purpose of getting ideas for Christian songs.

One day in March 1912, Miles, while developing film and waiting for the process to complete, picked up his Bible. It had fallen open to John, chapter 20. He found in that chapter the story of Mary's coming to the garden to visit the tomb of Jesus. As she looked into the tomb her heart sank because He wasn't there. He, standing nearby, spoke to her and she recognized Him. Her heart leaped for joy!"

Miles imagined that he was present with them in the garden on that glorious occasion, witnessing the wonderful event. When his thoughts returned to the business at hand in the darkroom he was gripping his Bible. His muscles, according to his own recollection, were tense and vibrating. Reverently he thought, "This is not an experience limited to a happening almost 2000 years ago. It is the daily companionship with the Lord that makes up the Christian's life."

In the inspiration of those moments he wrote a poem. He later said the words and phrases came quickly. That same evening he composed a musical setting, and in doing so gave to the world a song that has now become extremely well-known—"In the Garden."

I come to the garden alone
While the dew is still on the roses
And the voice I hear falling on my ear
The Son of God discloses.

Refrain
And He walks with me, and He talks with me,
And He tells me I am His own;
And the joy we share as we tarry there,
None other has ever known.

During his latter years C. Austin Miles often remarked that he would make it through another year if he could get through the month of March. He confessed that he did not like the winds that March often brings. Oddly enough, he passed away on March 10, 1946, in Pitman, New Jersey.

Reflection: Our joy is made perfect as we share that joy with others—the joy of knowing, in a personal way, the Savior spoken of in the Scriptures. When we turn aside to notice the plight of others, and to help, the joy of the Savior will overtake us.

22

A Wood Saw and a Sawhorse

What a Friend We Have In Jesus

We then that are strong ought to bear the infirmities of the weak, and not to please ourselves (Romans 15:1).

"That looks like a sober man, I think I'll hire him to cut wood for me." That was said of a man on the streets of Lake Rice, Ontario, Canada, as he walked along carrying a wood saw and a sawhorse. The response from a man nearby was, "That's Joseph Scriven. He wouldn't cut wood for you because you can afford to hire him. He only cuts wood for those who don't have money enough to pay." That seemed to be the philosophy and attitude of Scriven, a devoted member of the Plymouth Brethren Church. He had a sincere desire to help those who were truly destitute.

Joseph was born on September 10, 1819, in Ireland. His parents had financial means enough to afford a wonderful educational opportunity for their son. He was enrolled in Trinity College in Dublin where he graduated with a Bachelor of Arts degree.

In this young man, Ireland had the prospect of a great citizen with high ideals and notable aspirations. He fell in love with a young lady who was eager to spend her life with him. However, on the day before their wedding she fell from her horse, while crossing a bridge over the River Bann, and was drowned in the water below. Joseph stood helplessly watching from the other side.

In an effort to overcome his sorrow He began to wander. By age twenty-five his travels had taken him to an area near Port Hope, Canada. He became highly regarded by the people of that area. He tutored some of their children in their school work. It was there he met a wonderful young lady, Elisa Roche, and again fell in love. They had exciting plans to be married. However, tragedy reared its ugly head once again and she died of pneumonia before they could wed.

As indicated earlier in this story, he labored in Port Hope among the impoverished widows and sick people. He often served for no wages and even shared his clothes with those less fortunate than himself.

On an occasion when Joseph became ill, a friend who was visiting with him discovered a poem near his bed and asked who had written it. Scriven said, "The Lord and I did it between us." He thought the poem would, perhaps, bring some spiritual comfort to his Mom, who still lived in Ireland. Scriven had not intended that anyone else should see it.

On August 10, 1886, Scriven's body was pulled from a body of water near Bewdly, Ontario. Two monuments have been erected in his honor. Each has the first stanza of his song engraved on it.

Charles Converse, an attorney and composer, wrote the musical setting used today.

What a friend we have in Jesus
All our sins and griefs to bear!
What a privilege to carry
Everything to God in prayer!
Oh, what peace we often forfeit,
Oh, what needless pain we bear,
All because we do not carry
Everything to God in prayer.

Reflection: We must not neglect the opportunity, given to us by God, to talk to Him frequently about the needs of others and ourselves. We must continually draw on the strength He provides through communing with Him. Pray is the most powerful force available to Christians.

23

A Tragedy Inspired a Song

Stand Up for Jesus

Wherefore take unto you the whole armour of God, that ye may be able to withstand in the evil day, and having done all, to stand (Ephesians 6:13).

The year 1858 will long be remembered in Philadelphia as the time when tragedy struck, when great spiritual awakening came and when an exciting Christian song was written.

Dudley A. Tyng was one of the prominent leaders in this great period of history when men's hearts were turned toward God. He was speaking, early in that year, to a crowd of five thousand men, using as his text, "...go now ye that are men, and serve the LORD" (Exodus. 10:11). One report tells that men's hearts were so moved that at the close of the service at least one thousand men confessed Christ as their Savior.

A few days after that marvelous service, Tyng was at work in his study. For a few moments of relaxation he decided to walk down to his barn to watch a corn-shelling machine in operation. While he patted a mule, being used to operate the machine, the animal became frightened and leaped forward, knocking Tyng into the machine. This caused his sleeve to be caught in the cogs. Before they could stop the animal, Tyng's arm was pulled in and so badly lacerated that it had to be amputated. He lived only a few days after the accident. Just before he died, his dad, leaning over his young minister-son, asked him if he had a message for the young men with whom he had been working. He replied, "Tell them to stand up for Jesus."

George Duffield, Jr., a young pastor, and a close friend of Mr. Tyng, was so moved by that message he preached a sermon the following Sunday, exhorting his congregation to stand firm for Jesus Christ. His text was Ephesians 6:14, *"Stand therefore, having your loins girt about with truth, and having on the breastplate of righteousness."* At the close of the sermon he read a poem he had written:

Stand up, stand up for Jesus,
Ye soldiers of the cross;
Lift high His royal banner,
It must not suffer loss.
From victory unto victory,
His army shall He lead,
Till every foe is vanquished
And Christ is Lord indeed.
Stand up, stand up for Jesus,
The trumpet call, obey.
Forth to the mighty conflict,
In this His glorious day.
Ye that are men, now serve Him,
Against unnumbered foes,
Let courage rise with danger,
And strength to strength oppose.

There were six stanzas in all. Benedict D. Stewart, the superintendent of the Sunday Church School, had some leaflets printed for the children containing the poem. A copy found its way to a Baptist newspaper where it was discovered and later set to music which had earlier been written by George J. Webb.

Almost every hymnal today contains this great song, and it has found its way into the hearts of men everywhere—in many lands—causing them to have the courage to STAND UP FOR JESUS!

Reflection: As in 1858, our day needs men who are willing to stand up for Jesus—men who are willing to be leaders. Remember. . . when you follow the crowd you will not have a crowd following you.

24

Just Before the War Chariots

Peace In the Valley

But now in Christ Jesus ye who sometimes were far off are made nigh by the blood of Christ. For he is our peace... (Ephesians 2:13, 14a).

One of my prized possessions as a song historian is a 1977 recorded interview with Thomas A. Dorsey. I learned that in1899 Dorsey was born into the home of a black minister in Villa Rica, Georgia, a small town only thirty-eight miles from Atlanta. His mother, a music teacher, taught him to play piano as a child. As he grew into his teens he was drawn into the world of jazz music.

At age seventeen he moved to Gary, Indiana, pursuing a night club career. Two years later Georgia Tom, as he was known in his music world, could be found performing in the establishments on the south side of neighboring Chicago.

He was torn between the blues music and his Christian training. The stress was so intense he suffered a nervous breakdown and was two years recuperating. During that time he had become a member of the Pilgrim Baptist Church in Chicago, and began to play a major role in directing the music of the Church.

He wrote hundreds of songs, some of which were recorded by such notables as Red Foley, Connie Frances, Aretha Franklin, B.B. King, Jim Reeves, Roy Rogers, and Tennessee Ernie Ford.

To God Be the Glory

Dorsey said of the writing of "Peace in the Valley":

"It was just before Hitler sent his war chariots into Western Europe in the late thirties. I was on a train going through Southern Indiana and saw horses, cows, and sheep all grazing together in this little valley. Everything seemed so peaceful. It made me question what's the matter with mankind? Why cain't men live in peace?" Out of those thoughts came Peace in the Valley."

He later said he wrote the song for the famed Mahalia Jackson, known as the queen of Gospel. It has become extremely popular in America and far beyond our borders. I will never forget hearing a young, bare-foot black man strolling down a dusty road on Andros Island, an out-of-the-way part of the Bahama chain, singing Dorsey's "Peace in the Valley."

President Lyndon B. Johnson, before his death, requested that it be sung at this funeral. Anita Bryant was chosen to fulfill that request.

Oh well, I'm tired and so weary
But I must go alone
Till the lord comes and calls, calls me away, oh yes
Well the morning's so bright
And the lamp is alight
And the night, night is as black as the sea, oh yes
There will be peace in the valley for me, some day
There will be peace in the valley for me, oh Lord I pray
There'll be no sadness, no sorrow
No trouble, trouble I see
There will be peace in the valley for me, for me

Through phone contacts with his wife, Katherine, I kept tabs on Thomas Dorsey during the last months of his life. He died in Chicago on January 23, 1993.

Reflection: There is no word more precious than "peace," nor a more joyous state of being, for a Christian, than to know God's peace. We long for it, and when it comes to us it is directly from our Heavenly Father.

25

Washington Is Burning

The Star-Spangled Banner

Blessed is the nation whose God is the L*ORD; and the people whom He hath chosen for His own inheritance* (Psalm 33:12).

On August 13, 1814, the citizens of Washington, DC, watched in horror as their city burned. The White House, the Capitol, and most of the other government buildings were ablaze. England and the United States were engaged in the War of 1812.

As the British retreat to the ships anchored in Chesapeake Bay, near the mouth of the Potomac River, they took captive one William Beanes, a prominent physician and friend of Frances Scott Key, a lawyer and plantation owner. Key then secured permission from the government to negotiate for the release of Beanes. Although Key was successful, he and Beanes were detained over night on the British ship Minden. Their enemies feared they had learned of the intention to attack Fort Henry, near Baltimore.

While on board the ship Key and his party watched as darkness fell and obscured Fort McHenry, which had a fifty foot American flag flying overhead. They watched until the last gleaming of the twilight. A raging battle began. Cannon fire, rockets and flames allowed glimpses of the flag all through the night. As the day dawned "Old Glory" could be seen, still waving. They rejoiced that the Fort had stood.

To God Be the Glory

Key was so exuberant he grabbed an envelope from his pocket and began to write what his heart was feeling at the time:

O say! can you see by the dawn's early light,
What so proudly we hailed at the twilight's last gleaming?
Whose broad stripes and bright stars through the perilous fight,
O'er the ramparts we watched were so gallantly streaming.
And the rockets red glare, the bombs bursting in air,
Gave proof through the night that our flag was still there,
O say, does that star-spangled banner yet wave,
O'er the land of the free and the home of the brave.

Key finished the poem the next day in a Baltimore hotel room, adding several more verses. The original copy is in the Walters Art Gallery in that city. The poem, sung to an English tune known in the United States as Adams and Liberty, and written by John Stafford Smith, became so popular in our country that Congress made it our national anthem in 1931. The flag that flew over Fort McHenry is now on display in the Smithsonian Institute in Washington, DC.

Frances Scott Key, a devout Christian, believed deeply in liberty and freedom. It is reported that the slaves he inherited from his wealthy father were freed by him in 1817. Before their release he helped them with family problems, defended them in the courts, at no cost, and started Sunday school classes in order for them to be taught the Bible. He did everything in his power to lighten their burdens. He died on January 11, 1843. Two statues of Key stand in our nation, one over his grave and another in Golden Gate Park, San Francisco, California. A United States flag, by order of the government, flies continuously over Key's burial place in Frederick, Maryland.

Reflection: Who is the author of liberty? Who is the founder of freedom? You and I can never really be free—free from the guilt of our sins—apart from the freedom that Christ purchased with His blood on Calvary's cross.

26

Near Paul Revere's Ride

My Country, 'Tis of Thee

If the Son therefore shall make you free, you shall be free indeed (John 8:36).

There are songs which very nearly sing themselves—songs that unite our minds and hearts, and in a matter of minutes transport us to a lofty place and another time. Such is the song chosen to be the subject of this story.

Samuel Francis Smith, age 24, was thrilled as he heard a children's choir at Park Street Church in Boston sing, for the first time in public, a song he had written several months earlier. The presentation was on July 4, 1832.

One afternoon Samuel, a student at Andover Theological Seminary in Andover, Massachusetts, was sitting in his room on the campus. The school was near the church in which the lantern was hung during Paul Revere's famous ride. Lowell Mason, a music publisher, had given young Samuel, who spoke several languages, a number of European music books, asking him to translate some of the songs into English. Mason thought, perhaps, they might be used in a new hymnal being compiled.

As Smith began the task, his eyes fell on a German song entitled "God Bless Our Native Land." The tune had already been used in England for more than a hundred years as "God Save the King."

Instead of translating the original lyrics, Samuel decided to compose a new message for the musical setting. Thirty minutes before sundown he began the task. As the sun was setting, he wrote the last line, finishing what was to become one of the most famous of all American songs. He later declared that he had not intentionally tried to write a patriotic song, but it soon took on a life of its own. It served as our unofficial national anthem until the adoption of "The Star-Spangled Banner" in 1931.

To God Be the Glory

After graduating from Harvard and the Andover Seminary, Smith became a powerful minister in several churches in the East. He composed 150 hymns during his lifetime, and helped compile the leading Baptist hymnal of his day. He was also editor of a missionary magazine and spent considerable time visiting various foreign countries.

He passed away on November 16, 1895, while on his way, by train, to a speaking appointment in Boston. He was in his eighty-eighth year. Throughout his long and useful life he enjoyed many accomplishments, but none more significant and historic than the writing of:

My Country, 'tis of thee,
Sweet land of liberty,
of thee I sing:
Land where my fathers died,
Land of the pilgrim's pride,
From every mountainside
Let freedom ring!
Our fathers's God, to Thee,
Author of liberty,
To Thee we sing:
Long may our land be bright
With freedom's holy light;
Protect us by Thy might,
Great God, our King!

In our kind of a day, when freedom and life in the United States is so cherished, most every one old enough to sing knows Samuel Smith's masterpiece. Each time it is heard we should thank the Heavenly Father for all of the blessings enjoy by Americans. Sing it bravely. Sing it proudly, and sing it with gratitude in your heart.

The tune was titled America, and sometimes the song is called by that name, but we more often and perhaps more correctly say, "My Country, 'Tis of Thee."

Reflection: One of the foremost blessings from God's hand which you and I enjoy is the freedom to live in America, "sweet land of liberty." Yet, our most cherished freedom is available to all God's children—the liberation from the bondage of sin.

27

Converted to Flag Waving

God Bless America

If My people, which are called by My name, shall humble themselves, and pray, and seek My face, and turn from their wicked ways; then will I hear from heaven, and will forgive their sin, and will heal their land (2 Chronicles 7:14).

Our nation's solemn prayer and rallying cry has become, "God Bless America." The song with that title has become one of the most beloved in our nation, particularly since the events of September 11, 2001. Following those events United States senators gathered on the steps of the Capitol building and sang "God Bless America." It has become a part of the seventh inning stretch at Major League Baseball® games, and is heard at countless other venues.

During an Armistice Day celebration in 1939, Kate Smith first sang this Irving Berlin song, launching it on its flight across the United States. It is reported that she hesitated at first to include the song in her program, fearing that she might be called a "flag waver." However she decided to include it and as a result became famous.

Irving Berlin, the author of the song, was born Israel Baline in Eastern Russia on May 11, 1888. Young Israel was exposed to music early in life: his father, Moses Baline, was a cantor in the synagogue. The family moved to New York in 1893 to escape the massacre and slaughter in Russia.

To God Be the Glory

By 1907 Berlin had published his first song. During the next fifty years he wrote hundreds of songs, including White Christmas and Always and, of course, God Bless America.

God bless America, land that I love,
Stand beside her and guide her,
Through the night with the light from above.
From the mountains to the prairies,
To the oceans white with foam,
Chorus:
God bless America, my home sweet home.
God bless America, my home sweet home.

More than any nation on earth, we are a diverse population, gathered from the four corners of the world, working together to make America a unique and unparalleled nation in which to live and move and have our being.

If you have ever had the privilege of approaching the United States through New York Harbor, "Lady Liberty" came into your view. This grand statue was erected just seven years before Irving Berlin's family reached these shores as immigrants. There is no message on any plaque in America that is more often quoted and which has a more solemn and significant intent:

Give me your tired, your poor,
your huddled masses yearning to breathe free...
Send these, the homeless, tempest-tost to me...

Irving was not a shallow patriot. He donated millions of dollars in royalties to worthy youth organizations in America. In his late years he was presented the Congressional Gold Metal and the Medal of Freedom. Irving Berlin died in his sleep at his home in New York City on September 22, 1989, at the age of 101.

Reflection: May God give us the grace and courage to stand in the "gap" for Him, and to be loyal and true to the "land of the free and the home of the brave."

28

Victory On the Other Side of the Tracks

I Must Tell Jesus

Those things, which ye have both learned, and received, and heard, and seen in me, do: and the God of peace shall be with you (Philippians 4:9).

When the roll of great preachers is sometimes called, the name of Elisha A. Hoffman is usually omitted. As men count greatness, this omission is justified, but E.A. Hoffman was nonetheless a mighty servant of God. Almost two thousand gospel songs and hymns came from his pen. During my study of hymnology, which has spanned several decades, I have found that ministers of the Gospel wrote thousands of hymns and songs.

He spent many hours in his study, but not to the detriment of the poor in the homes across the tracks. One day he visited a home of one of his parishioners in the hills of Lebanon, Pennsylvania. Sorrow and affliction were frequent visitors at this home, too. He found the mother in the depths of sorrow and despair. He quoted verses from the Bible that he thought would console her, but he seemed to be unable to ease her distress. Then he suggested that she could do nothing better than to take all of her sorrow to Jesus. "You must tell Jesus," he told her. A light broke across her face and she cried, "Yes! I must tell Jesus." So she did. After a period of prayer, she rose from her knees, a new person.

Mr. Hoffman left immediately with those words ringing in his ears. "I must tell Jesus." He went directly home with this inspiration and wrote:

I must tell Jesus all of my trials;
I cannot bear these burdens alone
In my distress He kindly will help me;
He ever loves and cares for His own.
Tempted and tried, I need a great Savior,
One who can help my burdens to bear
must tell Jesus, I must tell Jesus;
He all my cares and sorrows will share.

Chorus:

I must tell Jesus! I must tell Jesus!
I cannot bear my burdens alone;
I must tell Jesus! I must tell Jesus!
Jesus can help me, Jesus alone.

Few gospel songs have been so dear to me. The tune carries the verses so well. "Down at the Cross Where my Savior Died" and "Are You Washed in the Blood?" are two other favorite songs written by Elisha Hoffman that have "echoed across America for half a century."

Reflection: Sometimes we forget that God wants to help us even more than we want to help ourselves. He wants to be our friend—not a buddy or a pal, but a true friend. Remember, He sat where we sit. He was tempted in all points like as we are.

29

Harpooned by His Own Crew

Amazing Grace

But God...hath quickened us together with Christ, (by grace ye are saved) (Ephesians 2:4a, 5b).

The story of John Newton is truly the story behind "Amazing Grace." One would be hard pressed to imagine a blasphemous life equal to Newton's early years. Nor would you believe the account of his life had his own hand not written it.

Death took his saintly mother in July 1732, when John was thirteen days from his seventh birthday. Newton wrote of her, "Almost her whole employment was the care of my education. At not more than three years of age she herself taught me English. She stored my memory with many valuable pieces, portions of Scripture, hymns and poems."

After her death, and with only three years of formal schooling, Newton went to sea with his father, the captain of a merchant ship. From that day Newton began a decline into rebellion and degradation that lasted until his twenty-fourth year. His willful and wanton disregard for all that is right and holy led him into a life plagued with despair, dangers at sea, abuse, public floggings, destitution, depression, near drowning and miraculous escapes.

During those years Newton often entered a state of spiritual awakening. However, those times were short-lived, and he invariably lapsed into a more wicked and loathsome lifestyle.

To God Be the Glory

While still a very young man he became the captain of a slave ship, landing at least one load of his human cargo in Charleston, South Carolina. It is reported that he often was so wretched his ship's crew regarded him as little more than an animal. He seemed oblivious to the plight of the poor black souls chained in the hold of his ship. Once, in a drunken stupor, he fell overboard and his ship's crew refused to drop a boat to him. Instead they threw a harpoon at him, hitting him in the hip. With it they dragged him back on board. Each step he took from that day forward was with a limp, a reminder of those difficult early years.

Shortly after a very harrowing experience at sea, Newton became ill, burning with fever, miserable and listless. He wrote: "Weak and almost delirious, I arose from my bed and crept to a secluded part of the island: there I found a renewed liberty to pray. I made no more resolves, but cast myself before the Lord to do with me as He should please. I was enabled to hope and believe in a crucified Savior. The burden was removed from my conscience." From that hour, according to his autobiography, Newton began to improve, both physically and spiritually.

Two years later Newton and his teenage sweetheart were married. During the following fourteen years, he continued studying for the ministry, and at age thirty-nine became a pastor in Olney, England. In 1779 he published a collection, "The Olney Hymns," in which he placed 281 of his own poems, including what is now the lyrics to "Amazing Grace." John Newton died in 1807 at age 82.

In earlier years Newton's verses were sung to many different tunes. The melody, so familiar to many, is a traditional American melody published in 1831. John P. Rees wrote the last stanza.

Amazing Grace
how sweet the sound,
that saved a wretch like me,
I once was lost but now am found,
was blind, but now I see.

The author of this story has written a Gospel tract based on this story. More than ten million copies have been distributed and has been a tremendous encouragement to many.

Reflection: The famous hymn writer experienced the miracle of "amazing grace" in profound fashion. You, too, can experience that grace!

30

We Wept as We Heard the Song

Give Thanks

Giving thanks always for all things unto God and the Father in the name of our Lord Jesus Christ (Ephesians 5:20).

Henry Smith, Jr., was born in Crossnore, North Carolina, in 1952, the son of Virginia and Eustace Henry Smith, Sr. He started piano lessons at age seven, but wanted no part of that. In his early teens, however, he picked up his brother's guitar, ordered from the Sears® catalog, and began to learn to play it. His teacher was the instruction manual that came with the guitar. His songwriting ventures started during those years and have lasted until the present. Of the nearly three hundred songs he has written, only one has been published—that's right, only one, but what a song! I was delighted with the following story he related to me during an interview.

"I had been writing a lot of songs, but in 1972, while a sophomore in college, the Lord seemed to increase His blessings as he poured out His Spirit upon me. Music for me has not been the same since that time. I only wanted to write songs for Christ.

"Six years later, in an apartment in Williamsburg, Virginia, I wrote the song, 'Give Thanks.' At the Williamsburg New Testament Church, where I was attending, the pastor had taught us from the Scriptures how Jesus became poor in order that we might be made rich in Him. I remember that some other Scriptures were woven into his lessons, making it a good background for a song.

To God Be the Glory

Give thanks with a grateful heart
Give thanks to the Holy One
Give thanks because He's given Jesus Christ, His Son
And now let the weak say, "I am strong"
Let the poor say, "I am rich
Because of what the Lord has done for us"

"Shortly thereafter, my wife, Cindy, and I, although at that time we were not married, sang the song at the church. We repeated it a number of times over a period of several weeks. There happened to be a military couple who attended the church for awhile who carried songs learned in the United States back with them to Germany. As far as I know that is how my song got to Europe. It did a lot of traveling before Integrity Music picked it up and published it. Now, more than 50 companies have recorded it and it has been published in a number of books."

A few years later, the Smiths attended a live Integrity Music recording session in Washington, D.C. At some point during the session Don Moen played a recording for the audience with Henry's song being sung in Russian. Henry said. "My wife and I began to weep. We were overwhelmed to hear my song in that language. Moen had no idea we were in the audience."

I think I can understand why so many people, worldwide, love this song. In the middle portion the "weak" can sing "I am strong!," and the "poor" can say "I am rich!," for the all-encompassing reason, "because of what the Lord has done for us."

In Uzbekistan, a country just north of the war-torn land of Afghanistan, a group of Uzbekies are singing a Christian song they recently learned. This is an unusual sight in a unique country. One photographer said, "Uzbekistan, crossroads of Asia, is an elusive mixture of Soviet industrial atheism, Islam and the Orient. Crossing the Kyzyl Kum desert in a Russian car left a lasting impression." The group is singing Henry Smith's "Give Thanks, "which had traveled from America to this extraordinary place.

Reflection: Every good thing with which we have to do, or which we possess, is a gift from our Heavenly Father. He wants us to be so grateful that we will "enter His gates with thanksgiving," and come into "His courts with praise."

31

She Wanted to Help

Just As I Am

Ho, every one that thirsteth, come ye to the waters, and he that hath no money; come ye, buy, and eat; yea, come, buy wine and milk without money and without price (Isaiah 55:1).

Evangelist Billy Graham was saved in a revival service held by Evangelist Mordecai Ham in 1934. At the close of the sermon Graham heard the congregation singing Just as I am without one plea... Is it any wonder that Evangelist Graham chose that song to be sung during the time he invited people to "come to Christ" in his evangelist services.

Probably the most widely-used gospel song in America today is "Just As I Am." It has been called the world's greatest soul-winning hymn and many souls have been influenced by the singing of it to give their hearts and lives to Christ. A complete volume could be written telling of the wonderful happenings in connection with the singing of this song.

The song's author, Charlotte Elliott, most of her life suffered the ills of an invalid body. Many times her weakened condition caused her great lamentation. Such was the case in 1836 when her brother, H. V. Elliott, was raising funds for St. Mary's Hall, at Brighton, England, a college for the daughters of poor clergy. She wanted so much to have some small part, but was hindered by reason of her physical condition. Everyone seemed able to help but her.

To God Be the Glory

During those days she wrote a poem to encourage others in her condition. She remembered the words of a great preacher, Cesar Malon, who had talked to her fourteen years before. He had told her to come to Jesus, "just as you are." That admonition helped her to trust Christ as her Savior.

Charlotte's poem was published, without her name, and a copy of it was handed her one day by her doctor, the latter not realizing that she was the author. Tears streamed down her face as she read the six verses. Copies of this poem were being sold and the money given to St. Mary's Hall. She then realized she had a significant part in the building of the school.

Only eternity will reveal the blessings heaped on other lives by this song. She probably would have shouted for joy if she could have heard the following story. One Sunday morning John B. Gough, the famed orator, left his hotel and walked to a church nearby. During the service Gough was asked by a man next to him in the pew what was to be sung. To the orator the questioner was a piteous sight—a victim of a malady that had left him blind and twisted in body. The poor, sightless man joined the congregation in the singing of "Just As I Am." As they came to the words, "Just as I am, poor, wretched, blind," this unfortunate one lifted his sightless eyes to heaven and sang with his whole soul. Gough later said, "I have heard the finest strains of orchestra, choir and soloist this world can produce, but I never heard music until I witnessed that blind, twisted gentleman sing 'O Lamb of God, I come, I come.'"

Just as I am without one plea,
But that Thy blood was shed for me,
And that Thou bid'st me come to Thee,
O Lamb of God, I come, I come!

Reflection: If it were up to us, many of us would try to clean ourselves up before yielding our hearts to Christ. Truly He wants us to come to Him just as we are. He can do a better "cleanup" job on us.

32

Outside a Darkened, Quarantined Home

Near to the Heart of God

The Lord is near to all who call upon Him, to all who call upon Him in truth (Psalm 145:18).

This is a tragic story, and yet, a wonderful song was born during the human suffering and sadness told about in this narrative which took place in Parkville, Missouri.

Dr. Cleland McAfee (1866-1944), a Presbyterian minister, served for many years on the faculty of Park College, a church-related school. He also served as the pastor of several churches.

Unexpected problems or crises may come into our lives. We often cannot escape the pressures and shadows that accompany those problems. However they can be faced with spiritual strength that God provides. This is the message expressed in the song told about in this story.

When tragedy struck a family, it was natural that they would turn to Dr. McAfee, the pastor, for consolation. The affliction told about in this story came much closer to his heart and it was two-fold. In 1903, two of his brother's young daughters succumbed to diphtheria—dying within twenty-four hours of each other.

To God Be the Glory

The double tragedy broke Dr. McAfee's heart, of course. However, the situation was made even more difficult by the fact that his brother's house had to be quarantined to prevent the spread of diphtheria. People were unable to go inside to express their condolences—and the family could not be permitted to leave the house to attend funeral services. You might ask, "How could it have been worse?"

Dr. McAfee sat up long and late, pondering what he could preach on the following Sunday, and what kind of music he could compose to bring comfort to his family and the congregation. The wonderful, comforting hymn told about in this story was the outcome of his meditation. Dr. McAfee prayed for God to give him the right words to help his brother and his brother's wife. Then he felt inspired to write a song. The choir learned it at their regular Saturday evening practice. Then, they all went to the quarantined home of the Howard McAfee family, and sang the hymn beneath the darkened windows. It was shared with the congregation at the Communion Service, the next day.

There is a place of quiet rest,
Near to the heart of God;
A place where sin cannot molest,
Near to the heart of God.
O Jesus, blest Redeemer,
Sent from the heart of God,
Hold us who wait before thee
Near to the heart of God.

It has been more than a century since Dr. McAfee penned the words of this song, but people today find it as comforting as did the people of that earlier day. We, too, need a place of rest, a place of comfort, a place where all is joy and peace.

Reflection: Many of God's children find themselves in the throws of human tragedy. The place to find comfort is in the Word of God, and in the realization that His promises are true and faithful.

33

Peace in Unspeakable Sorrow

It Is Well With My Soul

O that thou hadst hearkened to my commandments! then had thy peace been as a river, and thy righteousness as the waves of the sea (Isaiah 48:18).

The following story is only understood as we consider the unfathomable mind of God:

Horatio G. Spafford was a successful businessman in Chicago with a lovely family—a wife and five children. The Spaffords were not strangers to sorrow and tragedy. They had lost an infant son in dead, and much of their business in the great Chicago fire. However, the Spaffords had learned that God was in control of every aspect of their lives. The Lord blessed them by allowing the business to flourish again and by giving them other children.

On November 21, 1873, the French ocean liner, *Ville du Havre* was crossing the Atlantic from the United States to Europe. On board were Mrs. Spafford and four of the children, looking forward to a wonderful holiday. Mr. Spafford had stayed to care for some unexpected business problem, but intended to join the family in a few days on another ship.

About four days into the crossing of the Atlantic, the Ville du Harve was in collision with a powerful iron-hulled English ship, the Loch Eme. Suddenly Mrs. Spafford, her four children and the 221 other passengers were in grave danger. As the panic started, Mrs. Spafford hurriedly brought the four children to the deck. She knelt there with them and prayed that God would spare them if that could be His will, or to make them willing to endure whatever awaited them. One report says that she thanked the Lord that the children had become Christians just two weeks before.

Within a matter of about twelve minutes the ship slipped beneath the dark waters of the Atlantic, carrying with it most of the passengers, including the four Spafford children—Annie, age 11, Margaret Lee, age 9, Elizabeth, age 5 and Tanetta, age 2.

A sailor was rowing over the spot where the ship had sunk when he spotted a woman floating on a piece of the wreckage. It was Mrs. Spafford. He pulled her into the boat and they were picked up by another ship that landed them in Cardiff, Wales nine days later. From there she wired her husband this message, "SAVED, ALONE. What shall I do...?"

Spafford booked passage on the next available ship to join his heartbroken wife. With the ship about four days out, the captain came to him and told him that as far as they could determine the ship was near the spot where his children went down. It is reported that Spafford went to his cabin and, in his assurance that God is always good, wrote:

When peace like a river attendeth my way,
When sorrows like sea billows roll,
Whatever my lot,
Thou hast taught me to say,
It is well, it is well with my soul.

Chorus:
It is well with my soul,
It is well, it is well with my soul

Spafford later carried his poem to a brilliant young songwriter, Philip P. Bliss, who wrote a moving musical setting that has carried the song around the world. Bliss met tragedy himself, when at age 38 he died in a horrible train wreck.

Reflection: God will give us His peace when we meet His requirements. Many times He sends unusual circumstances into our lives to make us more like His Son.

34

A Teen's Christian Influence

My Jesus I Love Thee

...If a man love me, he will keep my words: and my Father will love Him, and we will come unto him, and make our abode with him (John 14:23).

A young teenager's masterful poetic message finds it way around the world. Occasionally in the search for information concerning the story behind a particular hymn obstacles are encountered. Such is the case with one of our best-loved hymns, My Jesus, I Love Thee. It was not until recent years that the identity of the teen songwriter, William Ralph Featherstone (1846-1873), became known.

It is reported that he probably grew up in Toronto, Canada, and it was in that city that he became a Christian in 1862. His conversion experience must have been extraordinary because soon afterward, and in connection with that life changing event, the sixteen-year-old wrote a poem which is still meaningful to millions of people in many lands.

Some historians have said that William mailed the poem to a relative in Los Angeles. From there it probably made its way to England in as much as it appeared in print in The London Hymnal, published in 1864, just two years following his conversion.

Years later, in Boston, Massachusetts, as Pastor A. J. Gordon was busy compiling a hymnal for Baptist congregations, he saw in The London Hymnbook Featherstone's "My Jesus I Love Thee." However, he was not at all impressed with the musical setting. He was a masterful pianist, so he wrote different music for young Featherstone's poem, music that has carried the lyrics to every corner of our world.

Following is an unusual story of a young actress and what this song meant to her. She told the leader of the troupe, with which she worked, that she had become a Christian and the lifestyle of show business was not what she wanted to follow. The director of the play persuaded her to carry through with just one more performance. All of the publicity had gone out and he had no other person to perform the part. She reluctantly agreed to participate one more time.

On the night of her final performance, immediately following the play she stepped quickly to the front of the stage and as the applause died away she lifted her voice and said:

My Jesus, I love Thee, I know Thou art mine;
For Thee all the follies of sin I resign;
My gracious Redeemer, my Savior art Thou.
If ever I loved Thee, my Jesus, 'tis now.

And she left the stage, never to return. The final stanza of young Featherstone's poem was:

In mansions of glory and endless delight,
I'll ever adore Thee in heaven so bright.
And say when the death dew lies cold on my brow,
If ever I loved Thee, my Jesus, 'tis now.

As stated in the beginning of this story the life of young Featherstone changed after conversion. He simply claimed the promises of God.

Reflection: If we love the Lord Jesus it will be shown in how we love others here on this earth. Jesus loves them and so should we. Much of our praying should be for others.

35

Choir Master of Lion King

My Tribute (To God Be the Glory)

For of him, and through him, and to him, are all things: to whom be glory for ever. Amen (Romans 11:36).

The Choir Master of the children's film, *Lion King*, wrote "My Tribute." Andrae Crouch was raised in a godly pastor's home and had the Christian training of loving parents. He also had a wonderful relationship with his twin sister, Sandra, who called him her "womb-mate." He began to play the piano at age eleven, with no formal training.

In an interview in 2001, Andrae told me the following story.

"When I became eighteen years of age God called me to work in the Los Angeles Center of Teen Challenge, founded by David Wilkerson, author of the famed book, The Cross and the Switchblade. During my first day at the Center I came into contact with Larry Reed, half white and half Mexican, who had been released from San Quentin Prison. He was a totally radical guy, an atheist, who didn't want anything to do with the Lord. However, he began to really love my music, and finally became a Christian.

"As I was thanking God for those experiences at the Teen Center, I received a phone call from Larry Reed. He said, 'Hey Andy! This is Larry.' I kinda chuckled. He said, 'I had a dream about you the other night. I dreamed that you were going to write a song that is going to go around the world. It will be the biggest song you ever wrote, to this day.'

To God Be the Glory

"I asked, 'Well, what do I have to read?' He said, 'Read John, chapter seventeen.' In that passage Jesus said, 'Father, I have glorified Thee, now glorify me.' I read the passage and didn't feel any inspiration to write.

"The following morning I got up singing 'to God be the glory.' I asked myself, 'Where did that come from?' I then went to the piano and wrote 'My Tribute,' in about ten minutes.

"That evening I was a dinner guest in a home, and we sang My Tribute for about an hour. I told them about Larry's prediction, that I would write a song that would go all over the world. My host, Carrie Gonzalo, asked, 'This morning—you wrote the song we've just been singing?!!' I said, 'Yes, but it can't be that song!'

"As we sat there we read the Scripture passage in John chapter seventeen, which Larry suggested. "I have glorified Thee on the earth: I have finished the work which Thou gavest me to do. And now, O Father, glorify Thou me with thine own self with the glory which I had with Thee before the world was." I excitedly said, 'It's all about GLORY!'"

The song that Andrae wrote captured the message: To God be the glory, For the things He has done.

Andrae Crouch passed away on January 8th of this year at age seventy-two. He was the co-Pastor of Christ Memorial Church of God and Christ in Los Angeles.

Reflection: My our labors for Christ be in His Name, for His Name and to His Name.

36

Writing for Others

Count Your Blessings

In every thing give thanks: for this is the will of God in Christ Jesus concerning you (1 Thessalonians 5:18).

Gipsy Smith, a famous evangelist of yesteryear, said of this song, "Men sing it, boys whistle it and women rock their babies to sleep to it."

Johnston Oatman was a citizen of Lumberton, New Jersey. His dad was a local merchant and just happened to be the best singer in town, with a rich, powerful voice. Young Johnston could not sing like his father, yet he grew up wanting to make some musical contributions of his own. However, for a time he worked in the family business, but soon gave up those opportunities and began to study for the ministry. After finishing school and ministering for a while, he continued to hope that life surely held some other plans for him.

At age 36 he found that he did have a musical talent after all. He could write songs for other Christians to sing. So, every year some 200 songs flowed from his pen. He eventually had written 5,000 songs and in his musical compositions had found a way to preach the Gospel. People everywhere seemed to adopt one very special John Oatman song. Very quickly his lilting "Count Your Blessings" began its meteoric journey.

To God Be the Glory

All too often, in this great land of America, we seem to lapse into a state of ingratitude, taking for granted all of the blessings and comforts we enjoy. We revert into an attitude of self-satisfaction, expecting that peace and bliss will always follow us. During those times we should, with sincerity of heart, count our blessings.

In this story our attention is called to three things: a very special song, a delightful season of the year, and a wonderful celebration observed in America. Thanksgiving or Thanksgiving Day is a holiday that we celebrate on the fourth Thursday in November. It became an official Federal holiday in 1863, when President Abraham Lincoln proclaimed it a national day of "Thanksgiving and Praise to our beneficent Father who dwelleth in the Heavens." Thanksgiving is one of the major holidays of the year.

Johnson Oatman Jr. died in Mount Pleasant, New Jersey, in 1936. Through his songs he continues to minister to millions.

When upon life billows you are tempest tossed,
When you are discouraged thinking all is lost.
Count your many blessing every doubt will fly,
And you will be singing as the days go by.

Chorus:

Count your blessings, name them one by one.
Count your blessings, see what God has done.
Count your blessings, name them one by one.
Count your many blessings see what God has done.

E. O. Excell, the gentleman who arranged the melody that we use for "Amazing Grace," set "Count Your Blessings" to music.

Reflection: The most wretched beings known to mankind are the women and men who refuse to acknowledge the blessing showered down upon us from God our Father.

37

Loving the Indian Children

Awesome God

Let all the earth fear the L*ORD*: *let all the inhabitants of the world stand in awe of Him* (Psalm 33:8).

The scene was the Ryman Auditorium in Nashville, Tennessee. A great crowd had gathered for the opening of the Gospel Music Association's annual convention in 1995. The crowd was awaiting many of the recognizable names in contemporary music. The performers were in their best apparel, and this was to be an evening of worship. Each person on the program presented his or her musical offering accompanied by beautiful lighting and all of the special effects at their disposal. After several performances a man walked onto the stage and took his place at the piano. A choir was behind him. As the lights were going up, Rich Mullins, began to play, some thought somewhat prematurely. He was dressed in scruffy jeans and a flannel shirt and was unshaven. He scarcely looked up from the piano. He was presenting his signature song, "Awesome God." The music ceased, the lights went down, and Rich Mullins slipped away—out of sight. Such was this man.

Let me say before I go any further with this chapter that I do not have the facts surrounding the writing of Rich Mullins' song, "Awesome God." Rich went home to be with the Lord on September 19, 1997, before I could get his story. He died in a tragic automobile accident. But, my brief summary of Mullins' life is the story behind his song. His influence on Christian singers compel me to include this chapter.

To God Be the Glory

Our God is an awesome God
He reigns from heaven above
With wisdom, power, and love
Our God is an awesome God

Rich was born, Richard Wayne Mullins, in 1955, in a small community near Richmond, Indiana, into a Quaker home. One day when he was about five years of age, his mother said that he was in the room listening to his older sister, Debbie, practice her piano lesson. She became very frustrated after trying several times to play a song without making mistakes. In desperation she left the room. Rich climbed onto the piano bench and played the song perfectly. Mrs. Mullins, from another room inadvertently complemented her daughter on finally getting it right.

He attended the Cincinnati Bible College, and while there formed a band called "Zion," which played local engagements. Of course, he later became a major recording artist, and formed a band to tour with him. He called the group The Ragamuffin Band.

He loved poor children and spent his money for causes that benefited them. He lived the last two years of his life on the Navajo Indian Reservation near the Arizona, New Mexican border, working with poor Native Americans.

I also learned from his Uncle Dick, as Rich called him, that during the last years of his life, although he could have lived sumptuously, he only allowed himself a yearly wage of $27,000, which was the average wage for a man in the United States at the time. The rest of his money went to a foundation to help the children.

So, when you sing "Awesome God," may it be as meaningful to you as it was to its author.

Reflection: May you and I recognize that in everything, our Heavenly Father is omnipotent, omniscient, and omnipresent and beyond our ability to comprehend. Yet, this great God invites you and me to fellowship with Him.

38

Longing to Be Happy, Again

Come Thou Fount

Delight thyself also in the L*ORD*: *and he shall give thee the desires of thine heart* (Psalm 37:4).

It is an unfortunate turn of events when a young boy is forced to grow up without a loving father. Thus was Robert Robinson's fate. His dad passed away when he was only eight years of age. Robert was born on September 27, 1735, to Mary Wilkin and Michael Robinson, a customs officer, in Swaffam in the county of Norfolk, a market town and civil parish in the English county side.

To make Roberts circumstances much more difficult, his maternal grandfather, Robert Wilkin, a wealthy man, who had never reconciled himself to his daughter's lowly marriage, disinherited his grandson and provided an inheritance for him of only ten shillings and sixpence.

As soon as Robert was old enough, he secured a job as an apprentice to a barber. Even in his youth he endured the hardship of having to be the breadwinner for his widowed mother and himself. His formal education was limited. However, his knowledge was varied and extensive because he spent many hours in study. There was an adult-like quality deeply ingrained in him, and it allowed him to accept the responsibilities of adulthood, even as a teenager.

To God Be the Glory

As he grew older, he came under the influence of the famed evangelist, George Whitfield. On December 10, 1755, Robinson could not push from his mind a particular phrase used by Mr. Whitfield in one of his sermons: "Oh, my hearers! the wrath to come! the wrath to come!" He was wondrously converted and became a minister of the gospel; first, in a Baptist church, then in a Methodist church, and later in other denominations. In one location his congregation grew to 1,000 in attendance. Unfortunately, and for some unexplained reason, he became altogether unstable and unhappy. His Christian beliefs and training seemed of little importance to him. On one occasion, years later, he found himself the fellow passenger of a young lady on a stagecoach. It is reported that she began to sing to break the monotony of the trip. And what did she sing?

Come, Thou fount of every blessing,
Tune my heart to sing Thy grace;
Streams of mercy, never ceasing,
Call for songs of loudest praise.
Teach me some melodious sonnet,
Sung by flaming tongues above;
Praise the mount—I'm fixed upon it,
Mount of Thy redeeming love.
O to grace how great a debtor,
Daily I'm constrained to be.
Let Thy goodness like a fetter,
Bind my wand'ring heart to Thee
Prone to wander, Lord I feel it,
Prone to leave the God I love.
Here's my heart, Lord, take and seal it,
Seal it for Thy courts above.

As she finished singing the young woman asked Roberts what he thought about the song. His startling reply was: "Madam, I am the unhappy man who wrote that hymn many years ago; and, I would give a thousand worlds, if I had them, if I could feel now as I felt then."

Reflection: Cling to the happiness that God has sent your way, and be thankful to Him for the blessings afforded because of it.

39

Mom Cried and Dad Was Happy

On Holy Ground

Then said the Lord to him, Put off thy shoes from thy feet: for the place where thou standest is holy ground (Acts 7:33).

Geron Davis, born into a pastor's home in Bogalusa, Louisiana, in 1960, taught himself to play the piano as a very young child. In an interview he related to me: "I was raised around music. I started making up songs as a small child.

"When I was 19 years of age my dad was pastor of a church in Savannah, Tennessee. The church had progressed and grown to the point that a new sanctuary was needed. When we were about two months from the completion of a beautiful new church auditorium, my dad asked, 'Son, would you write a song for us to sing during the first service in our new building? I replied, 'OK dad.' Well, a couple of weeks went by and I had not written the song. My dad asked, 'Son, how about it? Do you have a song for us?' I said, 'No dad, but I'll write one.'

"He kept bugging me. I was like, 'Dad, just chill out, I'll write a song.' Well Saturday night came, the night before the first service in the new church building, and I still had not written a song. My dad and I were taking care of some last minute chores at the church and he turned to me and asked, 'Do you have a song for us?' I used a good ole southern term and said, 'No sir, but I'm fixin' to.'

To God Be the Glory

"I went into the new sanctuary, dimmed the lights and sat down at the new grand piano. I began to think, 'What do we want to say when we come into this building tomorrow, to have a service for the first time?' I began to hum a bit and softly sing some lyrics that were coming to me. As I began to write the lyrics they kept coming, about as fast as I could write. Within fifteen minutes I had finished the entire song. I then went home and to bed. Someone later asked me, 'Did you realize that you had written something powerful?' I said, 'Are you kidding, I was 19 years old, it was midnight, and I wanted to get to bed.'

"I'm the oldest of four kids. I knew that I could be a little bossy with the younger children, so I got Jeff, aged 17, and Alyson, age 11, up early the next morning and taught them, by rote, all of the parts to my new song. We sang it later that morning in the church service.

"My dad was happy because I had written a song for us to sing. My mom cried because she thought her kids never sounded better. The congregation responded unbelievably to 'On Holy Ground.'"

"On Holy Ground" has become very popular, even to the point that President Bill Clinton's asked that it be sung at his mother's funeral. Barbara Streisand, who was in attendance, was so moved by the song, she later recorded it and put it on her subsequent CD. It has been recorded by hundreds of soloists and singing groups.

Reflection: The goal that all of us should strive to reach is to live in such a manner that we realize we often are in a place where God can meet with us and teach us His instructions for our lives.

40

What a Picture! What a Scene!

The Lighthouse

Then spake Jesus...I am the light of the world: he that followeth me shall not walk in darkness, but shall have the light of life (John 8:12).

Each time I exit our little community and turn my car toward the oldest city in America, the most notable thing in sight is The Saint Augustine Lighthouse. It rises 165 feet on the horizon and for 141 years has been a beacon of safety for those in vessels on the sea. Knowing about our Lighthouse made the following story more intriguing to me.

Several years ago Ronnie Hinson told me the story behind his famous song, The Lighthouse. In their teen years, Ronnie, his brothers Kenny and Larry and their sister, Yvonne, often sang as a mixed quartet in their home church in Freedom, California. They became known as The Singing Hinson Family and were invited to present their music at various other locations.

Ronnie said, "On one occasion, in 1971, we were in a large, empty church building preparing for our next engagement as 'warm-up singers.' We had worked for hours practicing songs from the hymnal and were becoming exhausted and discouraged. At that point I said to the group, 'I am going downstairs to the boys' room. I'll be back.' While there I picked up a roll of toilet tissue and began to write song lyrics on it. I went back upstairs and showed the group what I had written. One of my brothers snatched it from me and threw it into the waste can.

To God Be the Glory

"As we continued to struggle in our practicing and preparation—it was nearing dawn outside—suddenly one of my brothers retrieved the toilet tissue from the waste can and placed it on the practice stand. He said, 'I have an idea.' He began to sing and we joined in. We, for the first time, sang 'The Lighthouse.' Suddenly it seemed to be as bright as noonday in that church building.

"The first time we presented the song to a live audience it was very warmly received. Some would say 'it took off.' At this point in time—some forty years later—it would be difficult to find anyone, among those familiar with Christian songs, who has not heard 'The Lighthouse.'"

There's a lighthouse on the hillside That overlooks the sea.
When I'm tossed it sends out a light That I might see.
And the light that shines in darkness now Will safely lead me o'er
If it wasn't for the lighthouse
My ship would be no more.

In the beginning of this story, it was stated that the Hinsons lived in Freedom, CA. Their town was relatively close to the Pacific Ocean. However, Ronnie had never actually seen a lighthouse, and was puzzled that the song caused such a stir. He decided to ride his bicycle from Freedom to the sea, to find a lighthouse. When he came near to the water's edge he parked his bicycle, climbed upon a sand dune and for the first time in his life saw a lighthouse—the Pigeon Point Lighthouse. He told me he just sat there and said, "What a picture! What a scene!"

Reflection: A Bible passage that is difficult for you and me to comprehend is John 8:12, which assures us that Jesus, our Savior, is the Light of the world. We, in order to be safe and victorious must walk in the Light.

41

Not Ready To Go In

Sweet, Sweet Spirit

...The effectual fervent prayer of a righteous man availeth much (James 5:16b).

Doris Akers, born in Brookfield, Missouri, on May 21, 1923, was one of ten children. She learned to play the piano by ear at age six and by age ten had composed her first song. Since early childhood she was called "Doe." When she was only 22 years of age, she moved to Los Angeles where she encountered a thriving gospel music community. Two years later she formed the Simmons–Akers Singers and also launched a publishing firm.

In 1958, in a Los Angeles church, Doe started a racially mixed gospel group, the Sky Pilot Choir, which featured African-American gospel music. People would drive for miles just to hear their song arrangements. The Smithsonian Institute that labeled her songs and records "National Treasures" later honored her.

When I interviewed her in the late 1980s, she related to me that one Sunday morning in 1962, while directing the choir at the Opportunity Baptist Church in Los Angeles, she said to her singers, "You are not ready to go in." She didn't believe they had prayed enough! They were accustomed to spending time with her in prayer before the service, asking God to bless their songs. She said, "I feel that prayer is more important than great voices." They had already prayed, but this particular morning she asked them to pray again, and they did so with renewed fervor.

As they prayed, Doris began to wonder how she could stop this wonderful prayer meeting. She said, "I sent word to the pastor letting him know what was happening. He was waiting in the auditorium, wanting to start the service. Finally, I was compelled to say to the choir, 'We have to go. I hate to leave this room and I know you hate to leave, but you know we do have to go to the service. But there is such a sweet, sweet Spirit in this place.'"

Doris explained to me, "Songwriters always have their ears open to a song. The song started 'singing' to me. I wanted to write it down but couldn't. I thought the song would be gone after the service. Following the dismissal, I went home. The next morning, to my surprise, I heard the song again, so I went to the piano and began to put it all down." She had written the now-famous "Sweet, Sweet Spirit."

There's a sweet, sweet Spirit in this place,
And I know that it's the Spirit of the Lord;
There are sweet expressions on each face,
And I know they feel the presence of the Lord.

Chorus

Sweet Holy Spirit, Sweet heavenly Dove,
Stay right here with us, filling us with Your love.
And for these blessings we lift our hearts in praise;
Without a doubt we'll know
that we have been revived
When we shall leave this place.

Doris Akers believed that God wants His children to pray. Her songs have circled the globe, aiding Christians of all nationalities in their worship of the heavenly Father. She passed away on July 26, 1995, in Minneapolis.

Reflection: Not very much worthwhile was ever accomplished apart from prayer. The greatest example for our prayer lives was Christ our Lord, who felt the need of fellowship with the heavenly Father and took advantage of the opportunity on many occasions that are recorded in Scripture.

42

A Small Macintosh and a Cyber Bible

Lord, I Lift Your Name On High

Let them praise the name of the L*ORD*: *for His name alone is excellent; His glory is above the earth and heaven* (Psalm 148:13).

"Lord, I Lift Your Name on High," written by Rick Founds, for many years has had the distinction of being one of the favorite worship songs sung in churches around the world. On several occasions, on Easter Sunday mornings on Crescent Beach near St. Augustine, Florida, I led crowds numbering as high as 5,000 in the singing of this wonderful song.

Rick was born to Doyle and Lorraine in Idaho Falls, Idaho, in 1954. As a young child he became fascinated with music, climbing upon the piano bench as a young child to explore the world of music. By age ten he was writing songs for his Sunday school class. He also developed a love for the guitar and honed his skills by playing along with the commercials on television.

Following college, he taught visual technology at Saddleback College in Mission Viajo, California, and lead worship in churches on the weekend. From that employment he went full-time into the Ministry of Music at a church in California and continued there for fourteen years. While there he wrote his now famous song, "Lord, I Lift Your Name On High." He gave me, in a recorded interview, the following account of the writing of his song:

To God Be the Glory

"The song was born out of a typical Bible study or devotional that I have, usually in the mornings. At the time I was music director of a large church. I had an office in the back of the building, as far away from everyone as I could possibly be. I would sit in my office and play my guitar while studying.

"I had a small Macintosh computer and a Bible on a disc. I would bring up the Bible on my monitor and pick up where I had left off the previous day. I went through whole passages of Scripture in that fashion. I developed a habit of playing my guitar along with the reading of the Bible on my computer screen.

"One particular day, as I was having my devotional period, the Lord impressed on my heart that his work on our behalf was a cycle of events—Christ came from heaven to earth, gave His life on the cross for us, was buried and three days later rose from the dead, went back to His Heavenly Father, making the cycle and our salvation complete. That, essentially, is the lyric of the song. I picked up my guitar and began to sing, 'Lord I Lift Your Name On High.'

"It is just a simple song, but it is what the Lord dropped into my heart. The whole song came quickly. I didn't struggle with it at all. I did, however, continue to work on the latter part of the song for another four or five days, before I felt it was complete. I then sang it for an evening Bible study. They seemed to love the song. At the time I had no idea that it would be so popular—I had simply written another song, much as I had done so many times before."

The song began to rise in popularity, and now can be heard in other countries, in many languages. Rick rejoices in letters received from other nations of our world.

Reflection: There are times when we should worship the Heavenly Father, simply for who He is. There are times when we should worship God, simply because of His holiness. And there are times when should worship God for all that He has done to bring us to Himself.

43

From a House Trailer by the Highway

I Love You, Lord

We love him, because he first loved us (I John 4:19).

By age twenty-four Laurie Brendemuehl had met and married Bill Klein, and the Lord had given them their first child, a little girl. Bill was a student at Central Oregon Community College studying Forest Technology, and... well, let me have Laurie tell you the story, as she told it to me:

"It was a dark time in my life. We had no extra money, no friends nearby, no church home and my husband was busy all of the time with his studies. I didn't drive, so I couldn't get away. We lived on a highway in a mobile home, so I couldn't even put the baby in a stroller and go for a walk. Our only neighbors were people long retired and tired of life. I was lonely."

"The only thing I was committed to was trying to get up each morning before our baby, then a toddler, and spend some time with Jesus. I knew that was where the 'life' was.

"The day the song came, I had gotten up early and was sitting with my Bible and my guitar. I realized that I didn't have anything in me to sing to Jesus. I was so empty. So, I prayed and said to the Lord, 'If you want to hear me sing, would you give me something that you would like to hear?'

To God Be the Glory

"I started strumming on the guitar and the first words came out of my mouth with absolutely no effort: 'I love you Lord, and I lift my voice to worship You.' I scribbled them on a piece of paper. Those words meant a lot to me.

"I wondered if I could play the melody again—if I would even remember. I played and sang the two lines again. They were still in my mind. The last two lines just followed as effortlessly as the first two had come. It was a gift from God that just wrote itself.

> *I love you, Lord, and I lift my voice*
> *To worship You, oh my soul rejoice.*
> *Take joy, my King in what You hear.*
> *May it be a sweet, sweet sound in Your ear.*

"When the Lord gives you light, it makes all the difference, and you keep growing."

Then Laurie shared with me this heart-warming story:

"The most meaningful time that I ever heard anyone sing my song was in the fall of 2000 while my husband and I were in a discipleship training school. Late one night in the dormitory I heard a baby crying. I slipped down the hall to the outside of the door just to pray for the baby, that it would be able to sleep.

"As I was praying outside the door, I heard the mother singing a song, but the little one kept crying. She then began to sing 'I Love You Lord,' and while she was singing the baby fell asleep. The mother had no idea that the one who wrote the song was just outside the door."

Reflection: Jesus said that the most important thing for you and me is to love the Lord our God with all our hearts, all our souls, and with all our minds. These are all interwoven with our worship of Him.

44

I Made Them Face the Wall

Shout to the Lord

Honour and majesty are before Him: strength and beauty are in His sanctuary (Psalm 96:6).

Singing commercials for McDonalds®, Kentucky Fried Chicken® and Coca Cola® were some of the activities which made up the early life of Darlene Zschech (Check). She was born in Bribane, Queensland, Australia in 1965. In an interview she declared, "I can't remember a time in my life when music wasn't a critical part of the atmosphere in which I existed."

She related to me the following experience. "When I was age fifteen, my Dad, my beloved hero, who had been attending church and recommitted his broken life to Christ, took his eldest child to a youth group called Royal Rangers. I attended for a few weeks, making friends, tying knots, learning about camping, teamwork and the code of life, and most importantly, the giver of life, Jesus Christ.

"My memories of a particular evening meeting are so clear—the irresistible invitation to receive Jesus into my life. My longing to be made whole overtook my limited understanding, and I got out of my seat and, with a couple of other young people, walked toward the leader. He led us in the most beautiful prayer I have ever prayed."

To God Be the Glory

However, by 1993, at age 28, she was experiencing frightfully "dark" days. The tax burdens were exceedingly heavy. She said, "There seemed to be no way out of the situation, save for the hand of God." So, as Christians are encouraged to do in times of perplexity and fear, she turned to the Word of God—to Psalm 96. During the reading of the Psalm her mind was completely centered on the Heavenly Father.

While thinking on those Scriptures she slipped onto the bench of an old piano her parents had given her when she was only five years old. Her hands fell on the keys and she began to improvise, not really playing anything particular. Suddenly she found herself singing a song which flowed from her heart and from the reading of Psalm 96. She continued to sing it, again and again. Her depression lifted and her faith and joy in the Lord returned. She had realized that the message of her song was true. It began: My Jesus, my Saviour, Lord there is none like You. All of my days I want to praise The wonders of Your mighty love. After she had finished the verse the feelings intensified and she sang on and on until she had finished the song.

She began to say to herself, "I think the Lord has given me a worship song." However, she was very timid about singing her song for others. An example of her shyness was demonstrated when she asked the church music director and his visiting friend to turn their faces to the wall while she played and sang her new song. She said, "My hands were so sweaty I feared my fingers would slip off of the keys." As she finished singing the men turned and assured her they thought her song was wonderful.

Darlene realizes the song was a gift from God. It has since been translated into many languages and has circled the earth. The first words of the chorus furnished the majestic title for the song—"Shout to the Lord!"

Reflection: When you and I come before the Lord, realizing that He made everything and that He has it all under His control, then we rest in the total assurance of his might and grace.

45

Singing Near Wimbledon Stadium

Come, Now Is the Time To Worship

But the hour cometh, and now is, when the true worshippers shall worship the Father in spirit and in truth: for the Father seeketh such to worship Him (John 4:23).

Brian Doerksen was born into a very musical home in Abbotsford, just outside of Vancouver, British Columbia.

I called Brian and asked him to give me the details surrounding the writing of his most famous song, "Come, Now Is the Time to Worship." He did so, and I pass it on to you. Tighten your seat belt!

"We moved to England and I became the Worship Pastor of Southwest London Vineyard, meeting in the Elliot School. I had no other place to live and no other job offers. I felt as if I was barely hanging on to my faith in God.

"One morning, within months of moving to London, I went for an exercise/ prayer walk, as I often did. I walked just to clear my head, to pray, to give my day to God, and to pour out some of my pain and my dreams. As I was walking through southwest London, very close to Wimbledon Stadium, I heard this line as clear as a bell, floating through the air, 'Come, now is the time to worship...' I thought, WOW!, the call of worship is being sounded all of the time and in all kinds of ways. God is reaching out to us as His creation, inviting us to come to do the very thing we were created to do. I was sweating, and walking, and singing that line over and over again, just sensing the nearness and the presence of God.

"When I got home I ran upstairs. I sat down at the piano and found the key of the song I had just heard and began playing it over and over again, trying to unlock, 'What is this song? What is this call that is going on?' How is He inviting us? Is He saying, 'Come, just as you are, come to me?' Suddenly I realized that I was in my own dark time, and that His call to worship doesn't just come to those who have it all together, that have no doubts, that have no darkness or hard experiences, but it comes to all of us, across the board."

Come, now is the time to worship.
Come, now is the time to give your heart.
Come, just as you are, to worship.
Come, just as you are, before your God. Come.
One day every tongue will confess You are God.
One day every knee will bow.
Still the greatest treasure remains for those
Who gladly choose you now.

"The song became like wings to lift me up from those shadows that had almost engulfed me. It was my private song for several days. I spent time writing and rewriting it. I made sure of every word. I tried it out on my wife. I then brought it to my church. Within weeks of teaching it to our congregation I began hearing reports of other churches singing it. Within months reports came of the song being sung in other countries."

Reflection: Oh that you and I were constantly in the mental and spiritual state that we, too, can hear God's invitation, "Come, now is the time to worship."

46

From the Son of a Slave

We'll Understand It Better By and By

Now faith is the substance of things hoped for, the evidence of things not seen (Hebrews 11:1).

Charles Tindley was born the son of a slave, Albert Tindley, near Berlin, Maryland in July of 1851. His mother, a free woman, Hester Miller Tindley, passed away when little Charles was only four years of age, and a year later he was separated from his father. When he became old enough, although his status was recognized as "free born," he was hired out to work with slaves. Little did the people of Berlin realize that a theological and musical giant was springing up in their midst.

God had placed within Tindley's breast a desire to excel, and by age seventeen he had taught himself to read and write. At this young age he married Daisy Henry, who bore him eight children. The young Tindley family moved to Philadelphia where he obtained a job as a "brick hod" carrying mortar and other supplies to brick layers. He later became a custodian of the John Wesley Methodist Episcopal Church, a church which was to play a major role in his later life.

He attended night school for a time and because he felt called of God to preach, he enrolled in a correspondence course from Boston School of Theology. Along with his other courses he studied New Testament Greek. He found a Jewish Rabbi in Philadelphia who would tutor him in the study of the Hebrew language. In 1902 he became pastor of the church where he had served as janitor twenty-five years earlier.

To God Be the Glory

The church experienced rapid growth and by 1906, had a congregation of 5,000 members. Tindley was an eloquent speaker who was heard enthusiastically by people of all races. In the early 1920s the church, which by that time had 10,000 members, built a new sanctuary which seated 3,200 worshipers. Over his protest the congregation named the new church the Tindley Temple United Methodist Church. His wife, Daisy, passed away in 1924, the very day the congregation entered the new sanctuary for the first time. Three years later he married Jenny Cotton who survived him.

Music played a major role in Charles Tindley's life. He composed gospel songs in his mind, and not having the ability to put them on paper, would dictate them to a transcriber. We'll Understand It Better By and By is one of several C. A. Tindley songs that found its way into the hymnals.

Trials dark on every hand,
and we cannot understand,
All the ways that God would lead us
To that blessed promise land,
But He'll guide us with His eye
And we'll follow 'til we die,
For we'll understand it better by and by.

Chorus

By and by when the morning comes,
When the saints of God are gathered home,
We will tell the story how we've overcome,
For we'll understand it better by and by.

Tindley died in 1933, at the age of 82. It is reported that approximately 5,000 people crowded into the church to hear the memorial tributes to this spiritual giant. Some had openly recognized him as a "Lincoln in Ebony."

Reflection: Tindley's songs were instruments of encouragement to those who looked for a better day. They pointed to the time of deliverance for suffering people—to the times "when the saints of God are gathered home."

47

Godly Determination in a Young Boy

Come Ye Thankful People Come

Giving thanks always for all things unto God and the Father in the name of our Lord Jesus Christ (Ephesians 5:20).

Life, liberty and the pursuit of happiness are three blessings often mentioned when the idea of thankfulness and the Thanksgiving season arises. They are the mainstay or the backbone of a fruitful existence, a life well lived. Of course Christ taught these things on a number of occasions as he reasoned with his disciples while here on this earth.

Without a doubt, some of the most despicable people on the face of the earth are those who will not allow themselves to be grateful for the many blessings showered down upon them daily.

Now, for the story behind one of the most well-known and joyful songs ever written on this wonderful subject. I'm sure you have sung it, or have heard this song many times. Now for the story:

"I do this day in the presence of God and my own soul renew my covenant with God and solemnly determine henceforth to become His and to do His work as far as in me lies." These astounding words of determination came from a lad only sixteen years of age, in England, in 1826. His name was Henry Alford. He came from a long line of clergymen. His father, his grandfather and his great-grandfather were all ministers of the Church of England before him. He, too, became an Anglican vicar.

To God Be the Glory

Henry Alford was born in London in 1810 and was reared in that great city. His first charge, after graduation from Trinity College, Cambridge, was in Wymeswold, Leicestershire. His gentle disposition, cheerful attitude, and sheer genius catapulted him to fame and high honor. He reached the top of his profession in 1857 when he became the Dean of Canterbury Cathedral.

He was a versatile man: an artist, an organist and singer, composer of verses, and a very talented speaker. His literary ability was climaxed with the completion of his The Greek Testament, a commentary of four volumes, which required twenty years of hard labor.

It is reported that he loved to mingle with the common man. He never seemed to lose his vision of the pit from which he, too, had been lifted. He was thankful.

While he was at Wymeswold, his first charge, and in the fall of 1844, the people of this hamlet decided to have a festival, rejoicing in the abundant harvest already gathered into their barns. For this particular occasion Alford wrote a song that has been sung, perhaps millions of times during Thanksgiving celebrations.

Come, ye thankful people, come,
Raise the song of harvest home.
All is safely gathered in,
Ere the winter storms begin;
God, our Maker, doth provide
For our wants to be supplied:
Come to God's own temple, come,
Raise the song of harvest-home.

After you sing this inspiring song, rededicate yourself to a life of thankfulness. Learn to see and appreciate the little things that we so often overlook. Try this: Talk to God for fifteen minutes, thanking Him, and refraining from asking anything for yourself.

Reflection: Learn to see and appreciate the little things that we so often overlook. Talk to our Heavenly Father for a few moments and thank him for the little things we so often take for granted.

48

Astounding Questions for Mary

Mary Did You Know

But Mary kept all these things, and pondered them in her heart. And the shepherds returned, glorifying and praising God for all the things they had heard and seen, as it was told unto them (Luke 2:19, 20).

Mark Lowry, a singer, funny man and former member of the Gaither Vocal Band, was born in Houston, Texas, June 24, 1958. He learned to love music as a young child, often singing as his mother, Bev, played the piano. In his teens years he developed a love for Southern Gospel music, especially the songs of the Singing Rambos.

Although he was offered a scholarship to a college in Jacksonville, Florida, he decided to attend Liberty University in Lynchburg, Virginia. His older brother had studied there. He graduated in 1980. After becoming a member of the Gaither Vocal Band, he grew to be one of the most recognized and popular individuals in Christian music.

Although not known as a songwriter, the following is Mark's story behind his famous song, "Mary, Did You Know," just as he told it to me:

"In 1984 I was living in Houston and Dr. Jerry Falwell called and asked me to write the program for their next Living Christmas Tree. I had never done anything like that before, but anything he would ask me to do I would try, if for no other reason, just to see if I could do it.

To God Be the Glory

"In a conversation with my mother, I remember she said, 'If anyone on earth knew for sure that Jesus was virgin born—Mary knew!' That was a profound statement to me and it stuck with me. She knew that her's was not an ordinary child.

"I began writing a list of questions that I would ask Mary if I could sit down with her. Not only questions about his life as a little boy and as a teenager, but questions such as: 'Mary, do you know what is in your arms? Do you have any idea? All of Heaven, all that holds creation together, and everything that holds you together is lying helpless in your arms?' That is amazing!'

"And so, a very popular song grew out of that list of questions that Mark Lowry would like to have asked Mary—questions such as, 'Did you know that your Baby Boy will walk on water, or give sight to a blind man, or calm a storm with His hand? The answers to those questions would be wrapped up in the fact that He was and 'is the great I AM!'"

Mark had asked a number of musicians to write a proper musical setting for it, but none seemed to satisfy. In 1991 he asked the same of his good friend, Buddy Green, who wrote the beautiful melody that we hear today. When Buddy sang it to him on the phone. Mark's simple reply was, "That's it."

Reflection: Though different from the questions Mark would have asked of Mary, there are some answers that we should settle in our hearts today—answers to such questions as, "Do you know the Baby Boy, who is also Christ the Lord, as your personal Savior?"

49

A Pastor's Gift at Christmas

Silent Night! Holy Night!

For unto you is born this day in the city of David a Saviour, which is Christ the Lord (Luke 2:11).

It would be almost impossible to live through a Christmas season on our planet without hearing the strains of this Austrian born carol.

In 1818 a band of roving actors were performing throughout the little towns and hamlets of the Austrian Alps. One night the players came to the tiny village of Oberndorf, near Salzburg, for their annual presentation of the Christmas story.

The play was scheduled for St. Nicholas Church. However the organ had been damaged and could not be repaired in time. The show was presented in a private home instead, and the church's Assistant Pastor, Josef Mohr, attended.

As Mohr walked home that night through the new-fallen snow, his path led him over a small hill. Looking down on the little village below, Mohr was deeply impressed by the beauty of the glowing scene and the majestic silence of the wintry night. His thoughts took him back to the first Christmas—when angels spoke to faithful shepherds on a holy night such as this—and a poem began to form in his mind. He would later title it *"Stille Nacht! Heilige Nacht!"*

To God Be the Glory

Arriving home, the pastor quickly penned the words that would inscribe his poem into history. He sincerely wished his poem could be sung at the church's upcoming Christmas service, but he had no music. The next day Mohr rushed to the home of his good friend Franz Gruber, a schoolmaster in the village and the church organist. When Gruber read the poem he remarked, "Friend Mohr, you have found it—the right song—God be praised! It is reported that Gruber composed a musical setting the same day he received the poem.

On Christmas Day Franz Gruber and Josef Mohr sang their new song to the congregation gathered in the little church. Since the organ was still unplayable, Gruber accompanied them on his guitar, and "Silent Night! Holy Night!" was first introduced.

Silent night! holy night!
All is calm all is bright,
'Round yon virgin mother and Child!
Holy Infant, so tender and mild,
Sleep in heavenly peace,
Sleep in heavenly peace.

A few weeks later an organ repairman arrived at the church. As soon as he finished his work, Gruber sat down to test the instrument. It is reported that the first song he played was his new Christmas composition. Deeply touched by the music, the repairman took a copy of the song back to his own Alpine village. There, a family of gifted Austrian singers, the Strasser Sisters, picked it up and began singing it throughout the countryside.

The Strasser quartet created a sensation, and the carol quickly became a European favorite. It was translated into English from the Austrian language in 1863 by Jane Campbell and made its first appearance in America in 1871 in Charles Hutchins' Sunday School Hymnal.

"Silent Night! Holy Night!" is as fresh and beautiful today as when it was first heard in the little Austrian town more than 170 years ago.

Reflection: At Christmastime let the wonderful message of this song stir your heart anew and afresh, as you join in thanking God for the virgin-born Son of God.

50

History Repeating

I Heard the Bells On Christmas Day

Glory to God in the highest, and on earth peace, good will toward men (Luke 2:14).

Never a poet put pen to paper with more skill in verse than Henry Wadsworth Longfellow. His ability to portray life in one of the most beautiful fashions ever devised—poetry—is illustrated in his masterful, "The Song of Hiawatha." Longfellow was a legend in his own lifetime. He is known in many circles as "The Children's Poet." In his last years, in many schools, his birthday was a holiday and school children were excused from classes.

Tragedy struck in his home on July 9, 1861. His wife, Fanny, was near an open window sealing locks of her daughter's hair in a packet, using hot sealing wax. It was never know whether a spark from a match or the sealing wax was the cause, but suddenly her dress caught fire and she was engulfed in flames. Longfellow, sleeping in the next room, was awakened by her screams and dashed in and was severely burned on this face and hands as he tried desperately to extinguish the flames and save his wife. He was burned so badly he could not attend her funeral.

He seemed to lock the anguish within his soul. Because he continued to work at his craft, only his family knew of his personal suffering. They could see it in his eyes and observe his long periods of silence. His white beard, so identified with him, was one of the results of the tragedy—the burn scars on his face made shaving almost impossible.

To God Be the Glory

Even the literary giant, Longfellow, needed the peace that only God can give to His children. With the loss of his wife, only two and one half years earlier, and the tragedy abounding in his own country, on Christmas day, in 1863, he sat down and tried desperately to reflect on the joys of the season. Although not a hymn writer, the poem that he wrote on that day was later set to music by Englishman John Calkin. The result is one of our most popular Christmas carols.

I heard the bells on Christmas day
Their old familiar carols play,
And wild and sweet the words repeat
Of peace on earth, good will to men.

As he came to the third stanza he was stopped by the thought of the condition of his beloved country. The Civil War was in full swing. The battle of Gettysburg was not more than six months past. Days looked dark, and he probably asked himself the question, "How can the last phrase of those stanzas to be true in this war-torn country, where brother fights against brother and father against son?" But he kept writing:

And in despair I bowed my head:
"There is no peace on earth," I said,
"For hate is strong, and mocks the song
Of peace on earth, good will to man!"

It seems as if he could have been writing for the present day, too. Then, as every Christian should do, he turned his thoughts to the one who solves all problems:

Then pealed the bells more loud and deep:
"God is not dead, nor doth He sleep;
The wrong shall fail, the right prevail,
With peace on earth, good will to men."

Millions of children and adults alike all over the world love this carol.

Reflection: Peace and good will shall one day come when the Prince of Peace shall reign. Peace in this life, for a Christian, is from within, not in an exemption from suffering.

51

He Kept Moving Forward

Angels, From the Realms of Glory

And suddenly there was with the angel a multitude of the heavenly host praising God and saying, Glory to God in the highest, and on earth peace, good will toward men (Luke 2:13, 14).

James Montgomery lived in Scotland in the latter 1700s. While still a small lad, his father and mother were called as missionaries to the West Indies. They thought it best that James be left in the care of a Moravian community in County Antrim, Ireland. As he grew older he was sent to a school in England. Unhappiness soon would overtake him. To add to his dejection, his parents died when he was only 10 years of age.

Because of bad marks in school, coupled with the fact that he was left with nothing, he was taken out of classes at age 12 and given a job in a grocery establishment. This, too, was short lived and he soon became little more than a vagabond.

When things grew extremely tough, in order to survive, he roamed the streets of London, and sold poems he had written. His wanderings took him to Sheffield, England where he gained employment in the office of a newspaper, the Sheffield Register. One can imagine how he felt when he was given the opportunity to help run the business and to write for its pages. The writing soon became tremendously useful.

To God Be the Glory

When James was only 23 years of age the owner of the newspaper, after having been jailed several times, was driven out of town because of his open stand in favor of Ireland's freedom from Great Britain.

The newspaper fell into young Montgomery's lap. He changed the name of the publication to Sheffield Iris. He, too, took a strong stand against civil problems of the day and on more than one occasion found himself in jail because of things he had written. It was not easy being Irish under English rule.

The Sheffield Iris grew in popularity making Montgomery a wealthy man. At last, he had a place to publish his poems. He was also a great help to the community in that he became a supporter of the British Bible Society. The respect and honor afforded him made Montgomery a man among men in that town.

On the day before Christmas in 1816, and after reading in his Bible—Luke chapter two—of the heralding of the angels, Montgomery put pen to paper and by day's end he had written a poem that appeared in his newspaper the following day.

Angels from the realms of glory,
Wing your flight o'er all the earth.
Ye who sang creation's story,
Now proclaim Messiah's birth.
Come and worship, come and worship,
Worship Christ, the newborn King.

Henry Smart, a blind organist, wrote a musical setting for Montgomery's poem. The song was first sung in a Moravian Church in England on Christmas day in 1821. From that day forward the world has enjoyed the wonderful carol, "Angels From the Realms of Glory."

Reflection: God will mightily use those who are determined to go forward, in His name, even in the face of great odds.

52

A Rare Christmas Day

His Name Is Wonderful

For unto us a Child is born, unto us a Son is given...and His name shall be called Wonderful, Counsellor, The Mighty God, The everlasting Father, the Prince of Peace (Isaiah 9:6).

I have interviewed scores of songwriters, but no interview has been more captivating than the one in the late 1980s with Audrey Mieir of California. She has since passed away, but her songs live on in the hearts of Christians everywhere. She was a great composer, as well as a marvelous organist, pianist and choral director.

Audrey Mieir directed very talented choral groups, such as the Phil Kerr Singers, and also made herself available to small churches as well. It was in one of the small California churches that her most famous song was written. It all happened on Christmas day—one of those rare Christmases that came on Sunday. Audrey was 43 years of age at that time.

The "angel's" halo was a little crooked and the shepherds had their pants rolled up under their dads' bathrobes, but something wonderful was about to take place. A beautiful song was soon to be born. Following is Audrey Mieir's story just as she gave it to me:

We wanted to do something special in our little church, Bethel Union Church in Duarte, California. The pastor was my brother-in-law, Dr. Luther Mieir. We were using the young people in a Christmas presentation. Mary was a teenage girl and the angels were young boys. The baby was a doll. The whole place smelled of pine boughs, which we used to decorate the church. The atmosphere was charged. I so often have thought that I could hear the rustling of angels' wings. It seemed that the whole room was filled with the presence of the angels of God.

To God Be the Glory

I looked down at the little children and they were sitting there with open mouths, thinking, as they listened to the soft organ music. I looked around at the older people and they were wiping tears away, remembering many other Christmases gone by.

The pastor stood up and slowly lifted his hands toward Heaven and said, "His name is Wonderful!" Those words electrified me. I immediately began writing in the back of my Bible. As I wrote I was thinking that God has something he wants said. I wrote a simple chorus and I sang it that night for the young people around the piano. They sang it immediately. It wasn't hard for them to learn. I never dreamed that is would go any further, but it has traveled around the world in many languages.

She said of the writing of this song that she considered herself only a channel, and not otherwise involved. She gave God all of the praise and glory for using her to give the world such a praise chorus.

One day, some time later, she met Tim Spencer, a music publisher who told her that she had written a good song, but that it needed a bridge. At that time she didn't know what he meant. He explained to her that she could cause the song to be much more of a blessing with an extension to the chorus she had written.

She had been on her way to lunch when she met Spencer. While still in the restaurant's booth, during lunch, she opened her Bible and went over some names of Christ in the concordance, and wrote them down on a napkin. Later, in her office, she finished the song.

In her song she uses a number of the different names given to Christ in the Bible, names such as Wonderful, Lord, King, Master, Great Shepherd, Rock, Almighty God, and Jesus. She used all of these titles in her description of Him. The thrice-repeated phrase, "His name is Wonderful," in the beginning of the composition sets the tone and the spirit of the song, as it should be sung.

Audrey Mieir was born in Pennsylvania in 1916. She began her songwriting career at age sixteen. How thankful we should be that God chose to use her talents to praise Him with this simple and powerful song. She went to heaven in 1966.

Reflection: Why not make this song meaningful in your life today? Make the Lord Jesus Christ your great Shepherd, to lead your every step, the Rock on which you rest secure, and the "Master" of every area of your life. He is truly our almighty King.

Alphabetical Index of Songs/Hymns